ONCE UPON A WORKPLACE

A Christian Woman's Guide to

Navigating Toxic Workplaces

Monika T. Morrissette, MSW, LCSW

Once Upon A Workplace
A Christian Woman's Guide to Navigating Toxic
Workplaces
By Monika T. Morrissette, MSW, LCSW
© 2025 All rights reserved.

For permission requests, write to the publisher at:
SpeakTruth Media Group LLC
502 E. Houston Ave, Crockett, TX 75835
Email: order@speaktruthmedia.com

Cover design by SpeakTruth Media Group LLC in
conjunction with the author.

ISBN: 979-8-9884573-7-4

Printed in the USA

First edition: November 15, 2025

Dedication

This book is dedicated to all the Christian, Christ-centered, Christ-focused professional women who have endured, and who are enduring bullying at a toxic workplace, and who have said, "Enough is enough." This book is for those who have been humiliated, disrespected, dishonored, gossiped about, and dehumanized in the workplace. This book is also for the Christian Professional Woman who has sought to do things God's way and has been undermined because of the contrary, rebellious, controlling, manipulative, resistant, and narcissistic personalities, some of whom are leaders you have encountered. This book is for the Christian Professional woman who has been bullied and dishonored in a toxic workplace to the point that you have become stressed and are physically and emotionally suffering. God sees you, he knows you, and most importantly, he sees what was done and said to you, and He's fixing your Crown!

Acknowledgements

I want to offer my thanks and praise to my Lord and Savior, Jesus Christ, who reminds me that I am fearfully and wonderfully made, and He has not forgotten me.

I am thankful for the Helper, the Holy Spirit, and for the power of Jesus' blood. The same power that raised Jesus from the dead! Because he lives, I can face tomorrow!

I also want to thank my mom & dad, John & Linda, and my best friend, Michael, for all your love, support, blessings, and encouragement as I wrote this book. I love you!

Thank you, Mom, for always telling me to "hold your head high"! Thank you, Dad, for always telling me to 'trust the good Lord." Thank you, Michael, for loving me and encouraging me as I navigated a difficult season.

I am that kind of person who will give a shout-out to my dog. I am a dog mom, and I want to thank God for the blessing of such a smart, sweet, and feisty dog with a loyal and loving heart. She helped me through toxic workplaces, bringing encouragement and joy. I love you, Zoe Girl! Adopting a pet from your local shelter/rescue is truly a blessing from God!

I want to thank my friend, mentor, and sister in Christ – Charlana Kelly – who has spoken the truth in love to me, inspiring and encouraging me over the years to deepen my relationship with Jesus, stay close to God, and do things God's way. I want to thank Charlana for developing the Women of Influence Network, which has helped me grow as a Christian woman, professional, and leader. I have been loved, prayed for, and mentored, and as a result, I have grown in my faith and my walk with the Lord. I am genuinely grateful for the opportunity to be part of this group of women who have encouraged, prayed for, and supported me through life's and workplace challenges.

I want to thank my friend and sister in Christ, Gayla, who encouraged me to trust God as I went through what she called the "people test." I am thankful for her example and encouragement to seek healing at the root of strongholds and patterns in my life, to peel back those layers, and to heal. Thank you for recommending "Love is a Choice." Reading it changed my life and encouraged me to start my journey to heal. God placed some strong, praying, Holy Spirit-filled women in my life to mentor and love me through the toxic workplaces and life challenges I have endured. I am truly blessed, thankful, and living in God's divine favor.

Thank you to Phyllis, who helped me identify open doors to the enemy and assisted in closing those doors through deliverance. I am thankful for the good supervisors who wanted to see me grow as they developed and invested in me. I must express my gratitude for even the most challenging leaders, experiences, colleagues, employees, and workplaces. God has used what I went through for his glory. What you meant for evil, God turned to good. I thank God for the learning, growth, and refinement I received. I am thankful that God's word is true and that He never left me or forgot me. He helped me grow through and out of the toxic environments. I'm Thankful for the opportunity to share my experiences; nothing I went through was in vain. Thank you, Lord, for your many blessings and for being with me.

Thank you to the family and friends who have given a listening ear. Thank you, Darlene, for your friendship and cupcakes. You understand me! Thank you, Tandy. In case you didn't know, God used your gentle gesture of reaching out to check on me. When hurt almost made me think no one cared, and I wanted to hide and isolate. God used your kindness to show me He sees me and He cares. To my sisters in Christ from Women of Influence, you have seen my tears, accepted me, comforted me, and celebrated with me. I love you all! To colleagues and supervisors who were not silent partners. You are people who God blessed me with over the year: Makeba, Kristy, Susana, Sally, Angie, Diane, Karen, Kathy, and Pastor Jane. Thank you for your genuine kindness, authentic leadership, investing in me, and your support. Thank you for your solid examples during a time I needed to experience it the most.

I want to thank Real Talk Kim; your one-liners helped encourage me at a low point in my life in the toxic workplace I was in. You made me laugh and smile, encouraging me to get up and not give up. You helped change my perspective. I thank you, Lord, for the "confused fans." I pray they have an encounter with you in the name of Jesus, and I thank you for changing their stony hearts to a heart of flesh.

Contents

Dedication

Acknowledgements

Introduction: Survive a Toxic Workplace
and Live to Tell About It   15

Part One - Navigating the Toxic Workplace

  1. Toxic Leaders & Counterfeits   35
  2. You Will Survive   51
  3. Training Ground   63
  4. 'F' Them   81

Part Two - Conflict with Yourself

  5. Patterns & Strongholds   91
  6. Mental & Physical Health   99
  7. Counseling or Therapy   111
  8. Second-Guessing Yourself   123

Part Three - Conflict with Others

  9. Assess the Situation   141
  10. Gossips, Busybodies & Mean Girls 171
  11. Silent Partners   183
  12. But They Are Supposed to Be
      Christians   197

Part Four - Exodus Prep

13. Bloom Where You're Planted   219
14. Swing Batter Batter Swing   237
15. You Can Do Hard Things   245
16. Hold Your Head High &
    Fix Your Crown:
    Your Call to Action   253

About the Author   272

Summary   276

Resources   280

Bibliography   284

WORKPLACE BESTIE

[work-place bess- tee] (noun)

So, what's a "workplace bestie"? 1. A co-worker turned friend who shares the same daily torture and understands you perfectly because of it, she "gets" you, and you "get" her. 2. A co-worker you mainly communicate with through the use of eye rolls, sarcasm, eyebrow raises, "that look", and covert texts during meetings 3. The one who will always go out to lunch, tell you the truth, search for the best snacks, take a walk, or grab a coffee with you at any time!

INTRODUCTION

Survive a Toxic Workplace &

Live to Tell About It:

How do you do that?

If you picked up "Once Upon a Workplace" because the title resonated with your workplace experiences, welcome to the club! The "I survived a toxic workplace and lived to tell about it" club. It looks like we've both been there, done that, and bought a few T-shirts! You know what that makes us? Workplace besties!

As your workplace bestie, I have the 411 on how to navigate the *hot mess* called a "toxic workplace." Perhaps you picked up this book in search of answers, and my hope for you is that you find them. I pray that the Holy Spirit would use the words on these pages to lead, guide, encourage, and inform you. Whether you have been through the experience of a toxic workplace, are right smack in the middle of one, or you sense some shifting going on in your workplace, it is not by accident you picked this book up. I want to be to you what I *didn't* have, a workplace bestie to acknowledge, validate, and encourage you, showing you the way through. I think we both know the only way through is Jesus. What does that look like, though? Keep reading because I am going to share the way!

You are a busy, intelligent professional with ambition and goals, eager to grow and succeed. However, you keep hitting roadblocks filled with drama, to the point where you want to quit and walk away. Is the drama attaching to you like a magnet? Does some issue or problem keep happening that sabotages your efforts? Are you burned out, looking for solutions, and continually looking to improve, yet you can't seem to resolve the problem? Perhaps you have also felt like you have a bull's-eye on your back, seeming to catch all the drama, attitude, nonsense, and foolishness from different people in various workplaces. There is a chance you may have experienced a season of moving from workplace to workplace, problem to problem, like Goldilocks and the three bears, seeking a fresh start in a soft, comfortable place to land professionally. Am I right?

You may also be asking yourself, *"What's wrong with me? Why is this so difficult? It shouldn't be this difficult. Am I the problem? Why does it seem that everyone is working against me?"* You may also be in a place where you are perplexed and wonder, "Why is this happening to me?" You might even be saying I've tried to be kind, assertive, hardworking, and even loyal, but nothing seems to penetrate the toxic personalities and workplace culture.

Often, it's an unhealthy workplace culture; sometimes, it's just rebellious, contrary colleagues who are insecure and controlling.

Keep in mind that as Christians, we have the Holy Spirit who guides us. Those who behave, speaking in any way without regard, are not being led by the Holy Spirit. What's more, they may not even have the Holy Spirit in them. Remember *"You will know them by their fruits"* (Matthew 7:16). The truth is, it may also be at times a bit of your stuff. Ouch! I realize that didn't feel good, but stick with me; I promise we are going to work through this together. It didn't feel good for me either when a dear friend spoke the truth in love to me several years ago, encouraging me to look deeper at myself. I sniveled and boo-hooed, but had to admit it was the best advice. From that moment, I was on a quest to uncover the root causes of all of my problems. My stuff, your stuff, is what we bring to the table, the good, the bad, and the ugly.

When you pursue the patterns in your life, you discover healing and freedom. Being honest with yourself is never a pleasant experience, but it's a brave and mature thing to do. I call "repeating patterns" strongholds. When you get to the root cause of the strongholds, deal with them, and receive healing, it will set you free, point you in the right direction, and get you back on the path. Proverbs 27:6 says, *"The wounds from a sincere friend are better than many kisses from an enemy."* Like a true ride-or-die workplace bestie, I aim to speak the truth in love because I want you to shift the workplace atmosphere wherever you are and wherever you go.

Let's get down to business. You have a problem; you need a solution because people, places, and things are tap dancing on your last nerve, and you are about to scream. I have been in that place many times, and I screamed too. *"Once Upon a Workplace"* is written based on personal experiences, sharing the mistakes I made and the wisdom I learned as a result. I want better for you. I hope you will be better, do better, and handle things even better than I did. When we learn, are prepared, and know what to look for, we set ourselves up for success beyond the toxic workplace environment. Sharing experiences as I wrote required me to be brutally honest, not only about how different bosses, fellow employees, and the people I supervised were horrible to me, but also about identifying my own issues. You might pick up a bit of a feisty attitude here and there. As one workplace bestie to another, my experience has been long but is still fresh in my mind. Oh, the drama!

This book aims to reveal what I have learned, so you can learn, grow, change your perspective, and navigate situations so they don't handle you.

Have you ever heard the term "Imposter syndrome"? The term, according to WebMD, is used to describe when you doubt your skills and successes. You feel you're not as talented or worthy as others believe, and you're scared that one day, people will realize that. I was not immune! Imposter syndrome kicked in for me at times. I questioned whether I had the authority to speak on workplace toxicity and how to deal with it like Jesus would. God confirmed I have a voice that the enemy has tried to silence. When you are a Christian in the workplace, there is always a demonic assignment to silence you. Why? Because we stand for truth. Nowadays, people believe so many lies that they either cannot distinguish the truth or do not want to know it. I went through it and have the dings to prove it, but I lived to tell about it, and you will too! Believing the truth will set you free. When you are delivered and free, you begin to heal.

Learning to navigate through difficulty to find a resolution, we first need to assess the situation and then acknowledge the issues. To grow, overcome, and heal, you need to examine all contributing factors, such as what was done to you, what you contributed, patterns that are on repeat, and anything you allowed or tolerated. While it isn't only your coworkers and supervisors, not even only you and your issues, you must remember there is an enemy of our soul, Satan, who looks to create division, confusion, rebellion, who uses weak-minded people who have come into agreement with him in some form or fashion.

There is something huge inside of you, and many times the enemy knows your weaknesses, hurts, and plans an assignment against you to wear you out so you'll quit. You are going to get free. Heck, you are already free by the blood of Jesus! You will become freer and heal from your past 'stuff' to hear God's plan for your life more clearly. The noise in your mind and emotions can hinder you from hearing God's plans and directions for your life. Are you with me? Hang in there! Be open to listening to the Holy Spirit and pursue it in prayer, surrendering to what He reveals to you. Because this is not only about your stuff, the Holy Spirit will also help you identify what is not yours. Surviving a toxic workplace means your shield is up to deflect the words and behaviors of those used by the enemy to kill, steal, and destroy. Make sure to put on the Full Armor of God daily!

All the drama we contend with can be overwhelming. The goal of this book is to provide you, my workplace bestie, with a solution — not a band-aid — but tools that point you to the spiritual weapons you have access to. Reading the Bible and staying consistently connected to Jesus will help you overcome toxic and ungodly workplaces, people, and strongholds. The Holy Spirit placed on my heart to tell them the poignant things. There are many things I walked through. I have selected some everyday experiences that I am certain you either will walk through or are already walking through. Stay encouraged; you can heal. Wait, you are already healed, delivered, and set free in the name of Jesus!

Remember to laugh, it's how we stay hopeful and cope at times when everything feels like it will fall apart. Finding a way to laugh or joke through the hurt helped me at times. Proverbs 17:33 says, *"A merry heart does*

good, like medicine, but a broken spirit dries the bones."
You may want to give up right now because the
pressure and weight of a toxic workplace are
crushing you. A new perspective can be
incredibly healing and liberating. Right now, as
you begin to read this book, like me, you have
likely encountered people in your workplace
story who were used by the enemy to shut you
up, take you down, and silence your voice. You
may have experienced firsthand
discouragement, rejection, hindrances, shame,
dishonor, and humiliation. The enemy knows
you have something super huge on the inside of
you, and he works to kill, steal, and destroy
what's in you by using his emp's, demons to try
and wear you out, because he cannot take you
out. As a daughter of the Most High God, you

are blessed and highly favored, but maybe you don't quite realize that yet. Not knowing our identity makes us easy prey for the enemy to pounce, and we often become reactive people and not proactive people. Have you felt so entrenched in battle in the workplace that the attack is so heavy? Battling people, places, and things is enough to wear you out. You are trying to maintain your Christian witness in an ungodly, toxic workplace, and you just respond the best way you can, and it never seems to stop. The people being used by the enemy know you are a Christian and that you are trying to maintain your witness, so they have put a target on you to attack you and attempt to silence you. Sad but true, welcome to the real story. I was raised to have a good work ethic.

The fact that you are reading this book means you have a good work ethic and are perplexed by how to behave professionally in such a toxic environment. Others seem to think professional behavior is optional. I hear you, and most importantly, God sees you. You are why I wrote this book. At the end of each chapter, I have identified "Some Things to Remember" as nuggets and takeaways to help you navigate through wherever you find yourself in a toxic workplace season. Sit back, my Workplace Bestie, and let's learn some lessons. This is a training ground!

The Bible says in Jeremiah 33:3, the Holy Spirit will show you great and mighty things. The Holy Spirit is your Supernatural Compass as you navigate toxic workplace drama.   I pray that *Once Upon a Workplace* is an answer to your prayer. God was not going to waste my emotional pain, nor the tears I cried as I navigated the hills and the valleys. Your pain has purpose, and your tears are valuable. This is not the Yellow Brick Road. I serve God Almighty, and his streets are gold. There comes a time to leave behind the yellow brick road of this world and its ways, and focus on what is eternal. There is more value in a path paved in Gold because it never ends its eternal.

PART ONE

Navigating the Toxic

Workplace

"Why won't you stay down?" asks the toxic workplace.

"Believe us! We have nothing but the highest disregard
for all your hard work – no, seriously!"

CHAPTER 1

Toxic Leaders and Counterfeit Professionals

"You can't turn on a dime, you lack leadership and management skills, I know I trigger you," and other dehumanizing comments.

There once was a supervisor who told me, *"You can't turn on a dime."* The workplace treated me like I was less than human. I was bullied. I had to ask why the bullies were mainly women; was it the field I was in, social work/healthcare? The Workplace Bullying

Institute mentioned in 2021, "women bully women at twice the rate they bully men," and 40 % of managers were bullied, and 52% of non-managers were bullied. They went on to share that 48.6 million Americans are bullied at work. Multi-tasking in the workplace is a code word for industrialization, where human tasks are performed at machine speed. It can also be a quick way for a person to be bullied and told they don't measure up. It's also a quick way to burnout. There is a problem with this thinking. I am a human being. We are not Rosie the Robot from The Jetsons, and still, for some reason, toxic leaders will demean you and tell you that what you are doing is never good enough. I believe the word "multitasking" has been cancelled. It is the thief of productivity and only creates workplace stress, and that is "no bueno" for an employee.

Another leader said in a meeting that my colleague and I should walk lockstep together, which was alarming. I'm all for unity, but this sounded like indoctrination to me. That is how people lose themselves in toxic workplaces. You have to have a standard and draw a line in the sand. I will not walk in lock step with people who are not aligned with what is right. I can still honor authority and not lose myself or compromise the truth. Hearing the word choices was a red flag. Yes, listen to the words used by these toxic human beings. There is always an agenda; lockstep is defined in the Oxford Dictionary as "a way of marching with each person as close as possible to the one in front, adherence to and emulation of another's actions." So, first of all, this was like this person was recruiting someone for "their army." Recalling this toxic leader with a Jezebel spirit, it was evident how she sought to control not only leaders but also those under their leadership. I am for the armies of the Lord, and I am in the army of the Lord, so warning bells of every tone sounded, and I just looked at this person and saw them even more as a controlling individual. We will discuss this further later, regarding understanding the spirit behind a person. I said to myself, "No way, I am nothing like you all, so I'm not going to be in your army." I am already in the Army of the Lord. I have been fighting here long before you arrived, and I have armor. What do you have?"

Difficult to deal with: otherwise known in other terms, "not a team player," what they are really saying is that *"you won't do what we tell you, and we don't like that."* You may be perceived as difficult to deal with in a toxic workplace. If they were used to you being a people pleaser and you stopped making things comfortable for them, you were labeled "difficult to deal with." You see nonsense and call it out or question it. I pushed back on things, but professionally and sincerely —not to be difficult. It also has to do with what they want in terms of compliance. They don't want anything else, even if you are speaking the truth.

So, how do you navigate toxic leaders? By knowing your gifts, callings, talents, limitations, and adapting if needed, honoring leaders, but never compromising. Its hard to walk that line with evil leaders. Do not wait for a toxic leader to invest in you, mentor you, or encourage you. Look outside your toxic workplace for anything of value and for Christian mentoring. A toxic workplace has nothing to give you but stress. You do not need to be anyone other than who God made you. You are good enough because you are fearfully and wonderfully made! God says so!

A toxic workplace can be devastating, kicking, crushing, and knocking you down. You always need to know what is good about you, what you do well. If you are not doing this, start doing it now. Keep a Kudos file and your own personal cheerleader file on hand. This is wisdom for when you need to present evidence of your skills and contributions to the organization, or when you must prove you deserve a raise or discuss it during a job interview. Even if you have limitations, it's okay. Part of being mature is being okay with not knowing everything, acknowledging your blind spots, and actively working to improve. Don't wait for anyone to tell you that you are valuable. Do not wait for anyone to point out your limitations; you should have some idea of what you struggle with. I would trust the Holy Spirit to show you. A trusted friend or loved one can shed some light; the keyword is trusted. Consider if it is time to hold, fold, walk, or run. Workplace Bestie, you have been through a lot, and you must pray about God's timing. Should you stay or go? Ask the Lord for direction, wait, and listen for his leading. I know it's hard, but you have to sit still to hear what God is saying to you and to discern the direction you should take. We'll discuss later in this book what an Exodus looks like in a toxic workplace.

My mentor, Charlana, shared several things about leadership that helped me navigate through toxic workplaces and how to deal with leaders who are not leading you well. Our work is as unto the Lord. We answer to the Lord even though in our earthly employment we have supervisors, managers, and other leaders over us. Keep in mind the following as you navigate a toxic workplace:

Pay attention, workplace bestie, the following are some dos & don'ts about being an excellent employee. Do your part and do it well.

Remember, our God is about order, not confusion. There can only be one leader. Stay in line with the chain of command. As my mentor taught me, the leader has been placed in that position, and we are to respect it, even if we do not like the person; we must always respect the order and the chain of command. That is doing things God's way. Why, you may ask, because anything else creates confusion and gives place to a contrary attitude and a spirit of confusion. Let that not be said of you. We are to follow the leader, but clearly, if that leader is asking you to do something against the will of God, you need to speak up professionally. We are seeing that we have to take a stand and, as the Bible says, let our yes be yes and our no be no. As Real Talk Kim says, "No is a complete sentence." It does not require explanation to make someone comfortable. Be aware of your behavior and interaction. Are you following the leader, or are you undermining and getting ahead of the leader? If you are, you are out of order. The leader has been charged with the task of leading. If you get in there trying to run the show, you are contributing to the problem, confusion. I had confusion on my team because I had some employees who did not want to follow the chain of command. They would get ahead, undermine, and, unfortunately, the leaders over me were responsible for this as well, as they would discuss pertinent issues with my staff and not inform me (confusion and undermining at its best). Tell me this does not make leading a team difficult when you have interference, disrespect, and dishonor from the leaders of the leader. I was taught to be a help to those who are leading and be a joy to lead. Unfortunately, many of my employees were not a joy to lead because they refused to be led. Do your best to be a reliable employee. Even if the workplace is not good to you, do your best until God opens a door for you to leave and move on. We are told in the Bible to do the things that make for peace, whatever is in your ability and responsibility to do, contribute to peace, not drama. Pray for your leaders, and yes, even if they are evil to you and even if you disagree with them. I told my evil supervisors that I was praying for them, and they knew it because I told them.

If you are a leader in a toxic workplace, I want to tell you that, in this day and age and in the current state of our world, the workplace reflects a slice of the craziness that our society consists of. You, my friend, will need to pray without ceasing. You need to come to work prepared, you have a target on your back because you are a leader, but you have a bullseye on you because you are a Christian. Satan wants to destroy Christian leaders, especially those who side with and speak the truth. Satan uses evil coworkers, evil employees, and yes, evil leaders to create fear, to control, and to silence you. Pray and put the full armor of God on and plead the blood of Jesus over yourself, the work you do, and everything you say, daily. Be a servant leader, pray for those you lead, even the ones whose behavior is less than classy; after all you know they need Jesus! If there is contrary, resistant, and rebellious behavior, deal with it in real time; it will be the elephant in the room until it is dealt with. If you are like me and did not have real tangible support in your toxic workplace from your leaders, as a leader, pray and seek God and ask God for strategy and direction. Remember, Christian leader, you are under a microscope and the evil people at work attempt to lay traps and play games to distract, to silence, and to trip you up. Why, so Satan, the accuser of the brethren, can accuse, humiliate, and silence you. They look for every error or crack in your armor. They really hope that after all of the nonsense they put you through, you will leave.

Hey workplace bestie, I'll let you in on a secret, I would laugh at how bewildered some of them looked when I would show up for meetings and I was asked, "Oh, you're still here?" Many of them were visibly uncomfortable. I've heard it said that their demons are irritated by the light of Jesus. I refused to let anyone push me out. I left the toxic workplace when God said It's time to shake the dust off and move on and I literally wiped my feet and shook off the dust and did not look back!

Some Things to Remember

- Any leader that would embarrass, humiliate, disrespect, control, manipulate, or lie is no leader; they are taking space and have a fancy title that's all there is to say, folks!

- People who think they trigger you and then trigger you to get an emotional response are sick and twisted. Pray for them, they need an intervention and an encounter with Jesus

- Let the insults roll off your back by washing yourself in the word of God, and know what God says about you.

- Do not collect a toxic leader's view of you, toss it like rubbish, chew the hay, and spit out the stones. Be teachable, not a punching bag. If there's anything you can get from them, take it; otherwise, hit delete, reset your focus, and move on.

Exodus 14:14 "The Lord will fight for you, and you

shall hold your peace."

CHAPTER 2

You will survive: Find your Fight songs and Battle-ready Scriptures

You will remember this song if you are a Gen X or possibly a Millennial. "*Sing Sing a song make it simple to last the whole day long, it doesn't matter if it's not good enough for anyone else to hear, just sing sing a song, la la la la la la la, la la la la la la, la la la la la lá*" (repeat). I prayed for God to put a song in my heart. Praise will realign your attitude quickly. When you play your song, make sure you have the Full Armor of God on too!

"Accentuate the Positive, eliminate the negative, latch onto the affirmative, and don't mess with Mr. in between." The folks mistreating you are, in the meantime, in the "in between" hallway folks. When it's show time, or time to eat, it is safe to say they will not be invited to the cookout! One, since you are reading this book, you are moving on to the finer things in life. Don't let the hallway people into your space. You know the ones that hang out and gossip and lie in the hallway.

God told me this year that He is doing a new thing, so this book is written from the place of "after." I hope that reading the last line encourages you. There is an after; this is only a season you are in. God has much more in store for your future. Remember, He gives you a future and a hope. Hold your head up, fix your crown, and allow God to heal, guide, comfort, and refine you for your next season.

I love the instrumental song Fight Song/Amazing Grace by The Piano Guys. I feel encouraged and empowered after hearing it. For me, the song means that because he lives, I can face tomorrow, I can continue to fight because the Holy Spirit puts a new song in my heart, and His amazing Grace will see me through. This song helped me. The other song, which encouraged me and made me laugh, was the song "Tubthumping." For those of you who don't know the song, it is not a Christian song; I'm only focusing on the most important lyric in that song. It says *"I get knocked down but I get up again you aint never gonna keep me down."* Oh, how true that is! No one can keep you down, not because this song says it, but because of the finished work of the Cross, because the word of God says Jesus has overcome the world. He is the lifter of our head. He puts a new song in our hearts; we can do all things through Christ who strengthens us. The instruction in the Bible of putting on the whole armor of God tells us we will go to battle, and we need all of what that armor gives us to fight the good fight of faith.

I recall a time when, unable to speak, hurt and frustrated, I could only play songs that encouraged me. There are many. I have songs that were on repeat so much that they probably burned a hole in my playlist. But I needed to fight, I needed to stay encouraged. You need to fight the fight of faith and stay encouraged. The Bible says he is the lifter of your head. When you feel like you are going to battle every day, you get discouraged. I was battle-weary and wanted to give up. I even got to a place where I almost... I said, I *almost* believed what others thought and said about me. The Holy Spirit is my helper. I decided to reject the lies and believe the truth of what God says about me. Many times, the Lord would wake me up at 3 am and speak a word to me or direct me to pray. Even when you are tired, when you hear God say, "Get up and pray," do it! I remember being so exhausted I could not get up, and I hit the snooze button, and I heard, "Get up and pray, now." I prayed in the spirit, sang praises to the Lord, and warred in the Spirit over the heaviness. I would walk around my couch in the living room, a symbolic gesture reminiscent of the Israelites marching around the walls of Jericho. The walls and barriers I was facing were going to fall just as the walls of Jericho did. I believed that. You must keep fighting the fight of faith even when it's hard. You might get some grey hair from the stress and nonsense, but it means you're wiser, not weaker. God gave me an experience where I felt his goodness, protection, provision, and blessing. You can have that too when you put your faith and trust in Jesus and plead the Blood of Jesus over your situation.

I was orienting a new employee, their first day, and this person said to me, "Oh, I didn't know we could have Scriptures in the office." I knew right then she was sent by the devil. My response was "This is my office." All those years and Scriptures up and this newbie with a demon in tow decided to question me; get behind me, Satan, the Lord rebuke you! I had Scriptures on my bulletin board because I knew I had a bullseye on my back at the toxic workplace. The new employee overplayed her hand; isn't that how Satan works? He always overplays his hand. I knew right then she had misrepresented herself, and I had second-guessed my initial inkling about this person. I'll discuss second-guessing yourself more in a later chapter. I did not listen to the check in my spirit about this person, mostly because I was unsettled. The distractions around me were tossing me left and right, and I was constantly undermined and mistreated at my workplace. As a result, I thought, 'Well, maybe I didn't hear right.' But this new employee, in their second interview, said a lie about me, and I knew when I heard it, it was subtle, but immediately, I had a check in my spirit. Workplace Bestie, please do better than me, never ignore the check in your spirit. I had to learn the hard way, and thank God he gave me the grace to get through. She mentioned in a second interview with my boss that I hadn't addressed something, and I thought, "Oh, that was a red flag," but I didn't know how to put it into words. I think I was just shocked. So, here's a bit of advice, my friend: stop being shocked or surprised by people's behavior. Evil is as evil does. I guess I thought naively no one could outright lie like that…yes, they can if Satan is using them, and oh, how this person was being used. However, I imagine that the Scriptures on my office bulletin board irritated the demons in this person, as well as the others who worked against me. What I thought would silence them irritated the demons that circled my workplace and the door of my office. I was going to the spiritual battlefield every day! The word of God does not return void. I put Scriptures on my front door at home, so that was what I saw when I left for work each day. I put Scriptures on the corkboard behind my desk, so every time someone evil and nasty came in, they would have to see those Scriptures as they attacked me.

It may seem that evil people appear to get away with everything, but they don't. Yes, they do look like it. I have worked in places where people have plotted and planned against me, and I had no idea, and some I was aware of. You already have to fight battles, and you will need some fight songs to help you through, especially when you miss the boat and second-guess yourself, but God sees, he is Adonai El Roi, the God who sees, God sees me and he sees you. I got to the point where I would say in response to people, "God, you saw that," "you see what they're doing."

For a complimentary PDF of fight songs and battle-ready scriptures, please email me your request to: onceuponaworkplace@gmail.com.

Some Things to Remember

- Encourage yourself and do not rely on that toxic workplace to encourage you

- Put your Scriptures up at home and at work if you are able, or find a creative way to keep them where you can see and read them daily.

- Get up and pray

- You set the tone and atmosphere in your place of work and invite the Holy Spirit into your workplace.

I'm not everyone's cup of tea, but that's okay, because a lot of people drink coffee!

CHAPTER 3

Training Ground
Promotion, or was it?

The leadership at one of my workplaces never referred to the leadership position I had as a promotion. Instead, they referred to it as a "change in role." It was never clear to me why you would not refer to someone entering a management role as a promotion. It was demeaning in my opinion, another way to show dishonor and disregard for a person, and treat them like they are nothing. Leadership will reveal your blind spots; you have not arrived. Your blind spots and unhealed places will be on full display. They refused to call it a promotion, but here is what I got from them instead.

Dishonor:

I did not realize until after I left that horrible workplace that I really had been dishonored through being publicly humiliated in front of those I was tasked to lead, which led to further disrespect, which led to an environment where I was consistently dishonored. I realized that familiarity breeds contempt. When colleagues/employees get too familiar with you, disrespect usually follows. Many of them were the silent partners. On the surface, they seemed nice and helpful, but they will never have your back. Remember that.

Others second-guessing you:

When you second-guess yourself, others notice that, especially those with a rebellious, arrogant Jezebel, contrary spirit. I did my best, but I needed to break the habit of second-guessing myself. First, the issue was with listening to me. I would not second-guess myself if I knew I was hearing the Lord. We don't listen to ourselves; we listen to the Holy Spirit in us, and we have to learn to be still enough to hear. I was not still enough; the enemy always brought mess to keep me constantly putting fires out, distracted, just wearing me out left and right with nonsense. You will have to be intentional about shutting out the noise. Looking back, I see that the distractions were all part of the enemy's plan to make me so weary, distracted, and overwhelmed in my feelings that I couldn't sit still to clearly hear him. The enemy also tried to provoke me to respond to these weaklings, who used to attack me at work. You may have heard the saying "Silence is Golden." True story: sometimes, not saying anything and letting them look crazy all on their own is good enough! The organization I was in was going through a huge shift, and the leaders did not handle the changes the right way at all. They had a *"let them eat cake"* mentality.

Accusations:

Working in healthcare is hard. It's where sick and hurting people go; no wonder the devil has infiltrated and made it one of the most mean-spirited systems I have seen. I have seen this in many workplace settings, in my work as a social worker. But healthcare can be a hot mess because you will have so many different personalities, and it always leads to personality clashes. I worked in places where people did not like me because I did not lie down and shut up. I made my concerns known and was punished for it. I was accused of being difficult, of not being a team player, of giving everyone a problem. What all these workplaces wanted was for me to shut up, stay in my place, and say yes, all the time. Workplace Bestie, we weren't made to just shut up and stay in the place others try to put us.

Unable to Trust my Team:

I was worried when I became a leader that the silent partners and those who gossiped behind my back were making me look bad. They seemed never to do but the bare minimum. I had one that would do what they wanted, over and over. I had another employee who would often sneak up behind me and change my work, and she got offended when I called her on it. Now that I was the manager, I set things up, but this person slithered in and changed everything. This person was being used by a demon to torment and harass me. She was just a fragile person whom Satan and his demons emboldened. Sad, but true. When you have experienced trauma, you find it difficult to trust others. We take things personally because of hurt and trauma from the past. This person said, "I know I trigger you." It was like Satan was taunting me. The nerve of her to say that to me. Again, Satan overplays his hand, and her comments were proof that the enemy of my soul was seeking to torment me.

Promotion comes from God; some workplaces would rather further dishonor and disrespect you by withholding any honorable recognition. It hurt them so deeply to acknowledge this as a promotion. Workplace bestie, here is another nugget. We all want or even need recognition, but we need to start learning to distance ourselves from needing or requiring the accolades of man. People are fickle; one day they like you, and next you are no longer the flavor of the week.

Since no one invested in me, I sought Christian mentoring outside the organization to learn what true leadership entails. What I found was the truth and people God had waiting to encourage me.

Rejected:

Not getting that job or promotion. Man's rejection is God's protection. I was not selected for a leadership position. Later, the position created for someone without my credentials was eliminated as part of the restructuring of the new organization. I could never have written this. Our God knows the end from the beginning, and I stayed safely in the shadow of the Almighty. So my promotion came from God; he put me right where he wanted me, closing some doors and opening others. I came to see this rejection as God's intervention on my behalf.

A bit of backstory. God told me I would not get the position, but to apply anyway. So I did. It was necessary for many reasons; I did not want it ever said that I was overlooked for a position because I did not apply. I confronted their nonsense every time I threw my hat in the ring. They tried to control the narrative about me, but I regained control by doing what God told me to do. I did not make their rejection of me comfortable for them. I trusted God. They placed someone in a position without the credentials I have. That was one way they dishonored, disrespected, and humiliated me. When you are rejected, it is God's protection for you; it's not meant for you to take on that lie that you are not good enough. Praise God, I had people who encouraged me as I went through this, but I am thankful I also decided to see the truth and not the lie. The Truth was that the enemy was all in that hot mess. The truth is, I ticked someone off in executive leadership; in other words, I didn't kiss enough tail or stroke enough egos to show them I would comply with their nonsense. I had people-pleasing tendencies, but could not be controlled, so that upset folks. They thought I was easy until I said, "Hold up, wait a minute." As long as you are a yes woman, shut up, stay in your place, be seen and not heard, you are safe; anything else threatens the human beings in big positions and fancy titles. They are so fragile, and the only way they can keep their stuff together and not fall apart is to deflect their hatred of themselves and insecurity onto someone else that they know will call out truth and nonsense.

Rejection is a wound, and after feeling rejected, you may resort to hiding and isolating yourself like a wounded animal does. I had to wake myself out of that. Thank you, Holy Spirit. I was trying to hide. I wondered if I decided to get a remote job to hide. The Lord opened a beautiful door for me when I left the toxic workplace. When you have gone through trauma or hurt, your flesh will cause you to hide, isolate, and withdraw. You know you must be careful; you can end up at home indoors all week working if you are not careful. My word of caution and exhortation is not to allow rejection to cause you to hide, to isolate, to push others away. I knew as a therapist that my isolation was not healthy. It almost got me;

I was feeling myself sinking into sadness. I

wanted to be friends with everyone, but I did

not like how others treated me. It just takes one

horrible human being whom Satan uses to

speak negatively about you and spread lies to

the point that those who don't even know you

don't like you or hate you because of what

someone else said. Unfortunately, in toxic

workplaces, we usually have more than one

individual used by Satan. Toxic people and

toxic workplaces thrive on maintaining their

nonsense, so anyone who challenges it becomes

a target, and that toxic person and or workplace

tries or works hard to ruin your reputation.

Mark my words, you will recover all. It is

written in the Bible that he restores the years

the locust has eaten. I declare that everything done in secret against you and or to attack and malign your character and reputation is exposed in the name of Jesus. I cancel this demonic assignment in the name of Jesus and plead the blood of Jesus over you and your workplace. Remember to use your words and your power and authority. We have been given power and authority to trample on serpents and scorpions and over all power over the enemy, and by no means will anything hurt you, Luke 10:19.

Some Things to Remember

- If you take things too personally, break off that spirit of offense; it will not serve you well, especially as a leader

- Remember, when you are leading, you are to encourage and motivate those you lead to do better. We can only help at the level they are willing to receive, and sometimes you have to speak the truth in love. You are not responsible for their reactions.

- Familiarity breeds contempt- be sure not to want your team to like you so much that you overcompensate and over accommodate, or you are too accessible, as in my case, it breeds an entitlement attitude laden with disrespect and contempt.

- Know you will not make everyone happy

- Rid yourself of needing or requiring accolades from people

- If you have been harmed, emotionally heal, leadership will expose your hurt and unhealed parts

- Promotion comes from God; if it has not happened, it may be God's protection, but a person or organization not hiring you does not mean you are not a leader or cannot lead.

- Someone's negative opinion of you does not make it true. Remember, opinions are like belly buttons, everyone has one!

- God sees the end from the beginning, we see and know in part, so trust God has a plan if you did not or continue not to receive promotions or opportunities.

- Pray about the closed doors and pray about whether you need to shake the dust off and move on.

"Forgiving other people who have wronged us or hurt us or embarrassed us is not easy. In fact, sometimes it seems impossible. But that is what God did for us and what He asks us to do for others." — Korie Robertson

CHAPTER 4

F'them...

The F is for Forgive Them

That's the Best Way to 'F'

Them!

LOL, Gotcha... Workplace Bestie, I know what you were thinking. That other "F" word, you know, the one you use when you are fed up and want to whoop someone's tail for messing with you and mistreating you. I will be transparent, I have thought it and said it…while venting, of course. Dear Lord, I repent and ask for forgiveness in the name of Jesus! To be very authentic, I thought of the time I could have had that perfect time to say just that to these special human beings who caused so much emotional and professional harm and trauma. All I wanted to do was go to work, do my job well, and do good things. Well, this one was hard. We are human, and we have days when we either handle things in our flesh or maybe even consider giving toxic human beings a piece of our mind! I decided I was not going to allow them to steal my sparkle, and don't you let a toxic person steal your sparkle either! I kept my feet planted in Jesus and his word; that's how I stayed sane and endured bullying and toxic workplaces. As a Christian, the Holy Spirit gets a hold of me and says, "Pray for them. Forgive them." I cried a river and an ocean because I found it difficult to pray for my enemies, those who hurt me. We must surrender to and obey what God has told us and how He has instructed us to live. We are to love our neighbor as ourselves. We are to pray for our enemies. Stay with me, Workplace Bestie; don't check out on me now. It is liberating to come to the end of yourself and do what our Father God has told us to do. He is working out of you the pain and hurt, causing you to level up and deal with your situation using the authority he has given you.

Remember the War Room. It's been a battle. All that anger, hurt, and pain is hurting me… and it is hurting you. Why would we give that kind of power and control to people with an open door to the enemy? Take back your life, your health, repent, and ask God to help you forgive. Workplace Bestie, take this seriously: if you don't forgive others, you will not be forgiven. All I can say is that I must forgive people several times a day. I also ask God to help me and the Holy Spirit to work in my life.

The result of unforgiveness is bitterness. You would rather be obedient to God than live in unforgiveness, putting others in my life on the hook as if they owe me. They may owe you an apology, but you may never get one. You need nothing from people who have harmed you. I pray that the eyes of those who have harmed me and those who have hurt you will be opened. And lay them at the feet of Jesus—Lord, I forgive them and another F-word, Lord, I forgive them by FAITH. I want to preface this by saying that just because someone apologizes and says, "I am sorry," or "I am sorry I made you feel that way," doesn't necessarily mean they're sincere. The sincerity is not for us to judge.

Understanding people and their behavior, along with the message behind their words, helps us recognize when people apologize out of obligation rather than genuine remorse. To say I am sorry, however, is authentic. This person is taking responsibility for their actions and truly is not okay with the consequences. I can work with someone who is sorry for what they have done. I apologize, type people, just let me know you are aware of how I feel, but don't feel any responsibility. I will separate myself from people like this. They have shown me they cannot be trusted to treat me decently. That last group, the one that says, "I am sorry for how I made you feel." It is a gaslighting statement; it owes nothing in the way of responsibility but attempts to put the blame and responsibility back on you. You will know them by their fruit.

Forgiveness does not mean we pretend something wasn't done to us. It might look like protecting my peace. You are not forced to hug or shake hands with anyone who has brought you harm. You can excuse yourself politely and firmly. I know people who have hurt you, try to make you look bad, and force themselves on you in public in an attempt to embarrass you. You do not have to allow contact with anyone who has caused harm, is unrepentant, and shows no changed behavior. Guard your peace, space, and anointing. We can forgive, but we must be wise about that person. A truly repentant person may choose to approach you with greater common sense and respect.

Some Things to Remember

- Surrender your need to be right

- Forgive them

- You may be right and they may be wrong, but do what God tells you to do anyway.

PART TWO

Conflict with

Yourself

"Check Yourself Before You Wreck Yourself"

A variation of a quote from Ice Cube

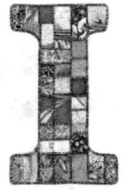

CHAPTER 5

The Quilt that Life Sewed: Patterns & Strongholds

First things first, Self-Evaluate: Let's start at the beginning, *a* very good place to start: Ask yourself these questions, and lift them in prayer for the Holy Spirit to shine his light and give you wisdom.

    A. How did you get to this place

    B. What are the patterns in my life

C. Where were things last clear and peaceful

D. Where did I see things change for the worse

E. Did you go down a path not meant for you

    1. We are all given talents and gifts. Am I walking in my God given gifts and talents? Do I even know what mine are?

    2. Do I feel I am drifting through life, and life is just happening, and it's not what I want?

Many of us struggle with second-guessing ourselves, our feelings, and our intuition. We don't need to rely on ourselves; we rely on the Holy Spirit to lead and guide us. Here are a few strongholds that you may be familiar with, which can hinder you in a toxic workplace: People Pleasing, Fear of Man, Comparison, Striving, Perfectionism, Feeling Inadequate, and Second-Guessing Yourself. These strongholds seem to trip up many people, myself included.

People pleasing:

This means we are looking to make others happy instead of focusing on pleasing Father God. Our priorities and perspective are skewed. Somewhere along the line, a lie was believed. We serve the Lord, and we are to work heartily unto the Lord. We are not to seek the accolades of man. Let me tell you how God broke this off me. People pleasing is an open door to the enemy, who uses other people to attack you in the area where you have an open door and strongholds. The need to be liked by others is frustrating. You may be frustrated, too. God helped me through this. Never being acknowledged or celebrated is extremely hurtful and makes one feel like anything you do means nothing. Others would be recognized, but some past supervisors, toxic leaders, would not recognize me. They would be quick to pounce and say negative things toward me. The people who couldn't speak kindly or acknowledge me, God showed me, were counterfeits from the enemy sent to discourage me. Many will also attempt to take credit for the hard work you do. It's as if they all colluded and didn't want to say a single nice thing. Better yet, they would say positive things in private and had nothing positive to say in public. So, I had to get used to others being celebrated and acknowledged and valued, while I just received criticism and insults. What did I learn? People are fickle; they change like the wind. Why would we focus so much on others? In Hebrews 13:8 NKJV, it says, Jesus Christ is the same yesterday, today, and forever. That's where we put our trust.

Never feeling good enough:

You need to resolve this first and foremost. Not feeling good enough will be a stumbling block to everything you do. If you don't feel good enough, someone in a toxic work environment will tell you what they think you are lacking or try to take away the little you value about yourself and stomp all over that. If you do not know your value and worth, seek the Lord, get that down, and get it from Father God first. You cannot wait for someone to tell you that you have value and worth, or you must know and be certain of your value & worth. The only accurate information about your identity, value, and worth is found in the Word of God. You need to know your value and worth, even if others treat you like you are worthless. Again, check and make sure you did not buy into the lie about your value and worth. People call it imposter syndrome. Workplace Bestie, you may feel at times that you do not belong; who told you that you did not belong? You may be taking on what limited view others have of you, or you may have bought into

Satan's lies via the weak individuals he used to tell the lie in the first place.

Some Things to Remember:

- Separate your who from your do: Your Identity
- Believe, declare, and decree the following over you and your life daily: *I will praise you for I am fearfully and wonderfully made; Marvelous are your works and that my soul knows very well.*

  – Psalm 139:14

Jehovah-Rapha- He is the Lord who heals!

"For I am the LORD who heals you."

– Exodus 15:26

CHAPTER 6

Mental & Physical Health

Two key factors in navigating and ultimately succeeding are your mental and physical health. When a person is stressed and struggling to navigate challenging situations and people, it triggers a stress response that affects their mental and physical health. My friend Gayla calls it the "people test." Physically, stress will affect your sleep, and when sleep is impacted, it makes coping with anxiety and depression much worse because you are in survival mode day after day. When going day after day to a toxic workplace, the stress and overwhelm will build layer upon layer with each day and each interaction until it brings you down and you feel anxious and depressed all the time. You're not alone; many people impacted by workplace stress and toxic workplaces have difficulty sleeping. According to PSHRA, "upward bullying does more than cause enormous distress to the target. It also impacts witnesses and drains an organization's resources. Decreased productivity, turnover, lack of leadership, poor morale, and higher health care expenses are among the costs of upward bullying for an employer. Over half of targeted managers report requiring medical treatment for emotional and physical health issues as a direct result of being bullied." PSHRA cited a study by Gemzoe Mikkelsen and Stale Einarsen in 2004, which showed the serious impacts of workplace bullying. It was found that "57 percent of targets exhibited symptoms of post-traumatic stress disorder." It was validating to find information about upward bullying. Managers are bullied as well. PSHRA also mentioned risk factors for upward bullying, and they shared the following:

"The strongest predictor of upward bullying is a workplace undergoing change or reorganization. When the status quo is threatened, employees may blame and act out against the manager. Other factors that may raise the risk for upward bullying include: an individual who is new to the organization or managerial role, highly

bureaucratic environments, a stressful work environment with unclear responsibilities and role overload for managers, and a culture where incivility is tolerated or encouraged."

This is not how God wants us to live. God's word says in John 10:10, *"The thief does not come except to steal, and to kill, and to destroy. I have come that they may have life, and that they may have it more abundantly."* I was weary of going to battle every day. There were times when I felt like my daily interactions with people, including executive leaders, supervisors, and colleagues, were akin to going to war. You know, like some of the battle scenes in movies like Braveheart, 300, and the Civil War movies. My goodness, stop and think, and tell yourself that you are still standing. You are still here! The Bible says

When you have done all, stand. I am still here. The enemy cannot take you out, but he used people to try and wear me out. All that constant stress will take a toll on you physically. Stress causes cortisol to go into overdrive in your body, making it difficult to regulate emotions and lose weight because it puts your body in a constant threat assessment. When you go into survival mode, your physical body follows suit. It's like burning a candle at both ends and not having enough to keep the flame burning.

The other important factor is your physical health. When we are stressed, in fight or flight or freeze responses, or survival mode, we go through the motions but are very emotionally disconnected. When stress affects your sleep, mental health, and physical well-being, you may start to neglect or overlook your own care. Lack of sleep may be one reason you are fatigued. You may have an autoimmune disorder or a condition that often goes unnoticed; you may have a nutrient deficiency. When you are stressed, it will aggravate any autoimmune issues you have, such as joint pain, hair loss, dry skin, high blood pressure, and just feeling unwell. Toxic workplaces are a health hazard, and they can cost you your health if you do not begin to take care of yourself. My experience is that I was exhausted all the time. I attributed this to stress and burnout from work, but I had been struggling with Anemia, and probably other key nutrients were missing as well. It was challenging to focus, concentrate, and interact with people. When you are stressed, you forget to eat and to drink water. These seem so very basic until you are in a stress response. No one at the job is diving in to save you. But Jesus died for you and took all of this on the cross. Stop what you are doing now and declare and decree that by the stripes and blood of Jesus, you are healed. Be sure to have labs run that can assess if you are deficient in key nutrients that help with energy, pain, and discomfort.

Burnout:

If you don't feel cared for, it's likely because you're not being cared for. You need to watch for burnout and be honest with yourself first. Ignoring burnout will only keep you a victim and hostage in a place that will not change. You need to understand first and foremost that a toxic employer will not take care of you. They will let you stay late, overwork, and overextend yourself while you fool yourself into believing those human beings will care or value what you do. They have you figured out; they know you work hard and will get the job done. They do not see the side that cares for you. When I left a prior job, I had nearly 2 months' worth of PTO in the bank. I took PTO, but often I didn't take enough, trying to "be present" while others frequently called out or took time off. Just as people will get used to working hard for the company, they will also become comfortable with you not caring for yourself. I cringe when I read that. No one should be used to you not caring for yourself. Workplace Bestie, please make a decision right now to show up for yourself, be your caregiver, and put yourself on your calendar like you would a doctor appointment. Stick to that. Do not cancel plans to make room for work events; you keep your word to yourself, too. You should enjoy the fruit of your labor. Just working and slaving away to please man; I learned that is ridiculous. People are fickle and are never truly pleased, but they will certainly use someone who aims to please them. Break that nonsense off you now, your life depends on it! The buzzword self-care is everywhere. I recommend saying it this way: self-care should not be another buzzword. Put hands, feet, and teeth to it by planning, making time, and showing up for yourself when it matters.

Some Things to Remember:

- Put yourself on the calendar or you won't show up for yourself.

- You are not optional, nor is your self-care

GROW THROUGH
what you
GO THROUGH

CHAPTER 7

Counseling or Therapy:

Self-Awareness

and Godly Insight

We all need someone to come alongside

us, help untangle things, give us feedback, and

assist us in processing the hurt, stress, and

emotional wounds we carry, which are

aggravated and exposed in toxic workplaces.

Let me be the first to say that if you are a

Christian, you should pray and seek God,

allowing Him to lead you to a Christian counselor. I will add that the first person we need to seek is Jesus. Pray about whether the Lord would have you seek therapy to help with your healing.

Very Well Mind, a mental health-focused website, regarding the Therapy article number 7092217, also mentions from the American Psychological Association that: Research shows that therapy can help reduce depression, anxiety, and eating disorder symptoms, as well as those struggling with addiction. In fact, studies show that about 75% of people who enter psychotherapy show some benefit. https://www.apa.org/topics/psychotherapy/understanding

This difficulty is for a season. Recognize the patterns in your life, be obedient, care for yourself, and the blessing will come. I have a great supervisor, and I connected with some great coworkers. See, we're not bad like they say we are. We know the truth; they don't, and neither did anyone who listened to gossip about me, who never got to know me; they just decided to partner with darkness, listen to, and spread lies. I have seen the good, the bad, the ugly, and the downright nasty, fake, and evil in leadership. But I have also been blessed with excellent supervisors and managers over the years. You must have bad leadership to appreciate excellent leadership. You can learn and thrive in a healthy environment. No workplace is perfect, but you are smart; you can distinguish between toxic and healthy workplaces.

Therapy/Counseling can help you identify thoughts, emotions, and beliefs that have led you to feel a certain way about yourself or your situation. It helps to have a trusted professional who isn't going to do some crazy, quirky stuff to help you get untangled in your mind. I recommend that as a Christian, you seek a Christian Counselor/Therapist, not one that dabbles in things that are not Biblical. You can find one close to you by going to the American Association of Christian Counselors and clicking the "Find Help" tab: https://www.aacc.net/.

Traumatic experiences play out in the workplace. So this is where we speak the truth in love again. I would love to say it's everyone's fault, but that is not how we grow or develop. We must look at ourselves and identify what is our stuff and what is not.

We have trauma from the past, and relationship dynamics that make us easy prey for wolves in sheep's clothing and for those who are narcissistic, controlling, or manipulative people given to the Jezebel spirit. When you begin to heal and the same witchcraft that made things so comfortable for people no longer works on you, then you will see yourself getting rejected and ostracized, gossiped about, no one will help you, and it will begin to look like everyone is sabotaging and working against you. People who cannot control you immediately try to control how others perceive you; they lie like a cheap rug. They help others but will not help you; they become contrary to everything. Again, if you are in an environment where you have been dishonored, it is just the perfect storm if you have any unhealed areas, trauma, or old wounds you have not healed from. You must go after your healing and do the work to release that pain and those strongholds so they do not hinder you from doing the work God called you to do.

No band-aids (for deep wounds), band-aids don't heal, they cover. I loathe Band-Aids; the symbolism of them bothers me. They do not promote healing; they cover up stuff so you can pretend everything is okay, and go on business as usual while you have been wounded. I do not like band-aid solutions because the problem keeps coming back. A leader accused me once of not being proactive. Interestingly, everything I did was proactive, considering the future. The issue is that they didn't like me and had to find an excuse to attack me. Deal with the wounds below the surface. Every bit of your stuff will come out when you are crushed and tested. When I was forced to do things I did not want to do, it triggered my emotions during a time when evil humans forced themselves on me against my will. So many times, we will have to acknowledge the truth about our stuff from the past that harmed us, which does cause us to be triggered. Still, in the bigger picture, the demons in the people who attacked, accused, rejected, and gossiped knew how to attack me because they have attacked me all my life; the enemy knows what we have in us before we even have the whole picture. In reality, there was an assignment, a hit if you will, by Satan, put out on me years ago. The attack began in many ways.

As you look over your life, where the enemy has attempted to shut you up and take you out, you will start to see the patterns. Do not ignore the patterns; they may be uncomfortable, but you need to know them to grow. When you know the truth, the truth will set you free. Additionally, when we lack knowledge, we also lack the wisdom to improve. When we know better, we will do better. One of those times, I could have died if not for the providential hand of God and the protection of the Lord Jesus. I am still standing here.

No band-aids for deep wounds. What does that mean? Well, you cannot cover it up, and when it comes to the surface, you had better deal with it, or like a weed, it will keep coming up, choking your beautiful rose garden. I am all for therapy; I am a social worker, counselor, and therapist. There can be many weirdos. Make sure you find a Christ-centered therapist who follows Christ and does not let worldly, new age, unbiblical matter enter their space as they are dealing with your mind.

Blind spots will be exposed, and as I have mentioned, you are under a microscope, especially if you are a leader. Remember,

Workplace Bestie, if you are hurting and have emotional wounds, let's focus on healing and working through that emotional pain. Your emotional pain is also worsening your toxic workplace experience. Get your healing and celebrate your deliverance.

Some Things to Remember:

- If you feel you are a few fries short of a Happy Meal, find a counselor/therapist and get yourself untangled, reset and stabilize your mental and emotional health, make it a priority.

- Find a Christian Therapist and be careful of pop culture new age stuff that is not Christ-centered and plays with the mind. You have the mind of Christ, your mind is not a playground.

- Talk Therapy with problem-solving, solution-focused, behavioral activation strategies are most helpful and avoid mind control techniques, for example, hypnosis. We do not want therapy creating new strongholds in your life or your mind. Remember, you want Christ-centered counseling/therapy.

Workplace Quote:

"The Worst part of a toxic boss is not just their behavior, but the way they make you doubt your own worth and abilities." - Balmy Quotes

CHAPTER 8

Second-guessing Yourself

Do you seem to discern incorrectly, or do you have that check in your Spirit, and do you choose to ignore it? That is second-guessing yourself. How do you feel when you are around others...when you first meet them?

We tend to dismiss these golden moments because we fear making a mistake, worrying about what others may say, or judging others. I say golden moments are the red flags that tell us exactly what we need to be aware of. We all need to work on perfecting this. Thank God for the Helper, the Holy Spirit, who will help us not second-guess ourselves. If the Holy Spirit truly leads us, then we are not trusting ourselves; we are trusting the leading of the Holy Spirit. That way, we will never second-guess ourselves in the first place.

As a counselor, this issue has plagued the majority of my clients I have worked with. It is rooted in you not trusting yourself, but even deeper, it is rooted in not trusting God. We have been given help here as Christians, called the Holy Spirit. We have the home court advantage of gaining access to unwritten rules, information, playbooks, and strategies before anything goes down — if we listen. Second-guessing is a symptom of anxiety and fear. You fear that you cannot trust your feelings, thoughts, and what you know to be true. Why, because we believed a lie. We are given the hints, the truth, and the warning, but we choose to dismiss them and minimize their significance. What we have done is dismiss the truth. When we second-guess ourselves, we base our decisions on several factors, including perfectionism, people-pleasing, and rationalizing our concerns. But when we second-guess ourselves, it means we've arrived at an answer and decided it's not good enough.

Do this enough, and you will have consequences to deal with.

I'll give you an example. I was in a toxic work environment, I was a leader and was not supported or encouraged, and forget about any decent life-changing mentoring. That is nonexistent in a toxic workplace. It was an environment that thrived on control and manipulation, and I seemed to always run into personalities that would put me down. You see, two things were going on. I was already struggling with second-guessing myself. The devil knew this, and so anytime God moved me into position, I would run into individuals with an open door to demonic influence who would berate and beat me down verbally. This did not encourage me to stop second-guessing myself.

Second-guessing yourself is the door left open for the enemy to creep in. We don't know the door is open, so attacks by the enemy keep happening repeatedly. Same issue, different faces.

What did it look like: Well, I had things meticulously planned out and organized, and then the second-guesser would usually be someone who made it clear they did not like me, did not feel they should listen to anything I had to say, or this person listened to and participated in gossip about me. Keep in mind, they learned this because leadership was never observed supporting me in any way. So, they acted out their manipulative behavior. They were given permission to behave in this manner. Workplace Bestie, does any of this sound familiar? Has this happened to you?

I would attempt to be professional, and individuals who did not like me, who always had a contrary remark, I call them pot shots; nothing ever came out affirmative or encouraging. They had to have something negative to say. It made it easier for them because I gave off the impression that I second-guess myself, so unfortunately, I was not hard to spot. This made me a target for controlling and manipulative people. The ones who made it their mission to trigger you daily. They are usually part of the mean girl brigade, operating with a spirit of harassment. I didn't see this at first, but I later realized it was my pattern. When individuals used my second-guessing as a way to control or manipulate me, I was aware of it. This awareness made me feel ticked off, which in turn led me to push back. Especially when leading, this pushback resembles a power struggle with those who refuse to follow the leader's direction. Power struggles continued to occur. This happened when I was a regular employee, but worsened when I became a Leader. The second guesser — well, I was warned about this person — but I second-guessed myself because I couldn't pinpoint what made me uncomfortable when communicating with them. But this person showed their true self, and I had a check in my spirit. I immediately got uncomfortable in the meeting. Because I did not know how to communicate my discomfort, I second-guessed myself. I wish I could tell you this was the only time, but no. Workplace Bestie, I had lessons to learn, and this was a doozy. It would have meant that if I had spoken up and said I was not comfortable with this person, it might have prevented them from entering my space. The devil knows what you struggle with, and if you are struggling with that issue, it is an open door for Satan to slither in with his demons. This person had many demons. I bet some people you work with or have worked with come to mind right now. Don't engage in second-guessing; proceed with caution. Full confession, I made the same mistake with another person, a few months prior, but God was gracious and removed this person, and they went on their merry way. But I had to face this issue again until I realized my pattern. I was so mad when I finally saw it. The world, secular culture, therapists are taught to "trust your gut." The Holy Spirit leads us. The word says the Holy Spirit will bring all things to your remembrance, John 14:26. As Children of God, we trust what the Holy Spirit says, and when we have a check in our spirit, that is a warning. In light of this truth, what did I learn?

I made a mistake, and I needed to repent for not listening to the warning of the Holy Spirit. Do you need to repent for second-guessing the leading of the Holy Spirit? Don't beat yourself up, Workplace Bestie, repent, ask for forgiveness, and seek what God would have you do now. Remember these important facts and personalize them to you:

1. God will help me and give me the grace to endure

2. I do not have to have it figured out.

I had to heal from my issues, or this pattern would continue. Focusing on perfection or being fearful of making the wrong decision causes us to focus on the wrong things. We need to learn to surrender and put our trust in the finished work of the cross. I could not trust myself, but I could and needed to trust the leading of the Holy Spirit. Second-guessing yourself is essentially relying on yourself without the guidance of the Holy Spirit, which means we are doing things in our own strength. If you sense something is off in your spirit and don't have specifics, but you know you do not have peace, your answer can be a hard 'no'. I worried about not having the right words or an answer to justify my 'no'. No is no, and my discomfort was telling me something I needed to pay attention to. Workplace Bestie, have you ever had or do you now have a check in your spirit regarding something where peace is absent?

The key to success is prayer: The Holy Spirit is your helper, and you have home court advantage. You are not in this alone to make decisions on your own. To avoid second-guessing yourself, you need to practice hearing the voice of the King of Kings, the Lord of Lords. This means you need time with the Lord to receive the strategies He gives you for dealing with the works of darkness in the workplace. I prayed: Lord, I trust you. I cannot do anything with you. Please give me wisdom and discernment. I surrender and lay this situation and these individuals at your feet. I believe and thank you that the same power that raised Jesus from the dead is the same power that will help me make the best decision. You may be asking, "How do we hear from the Holy Spirit?" You need to settle yourself and sit still. I realize that it is difficult in the most epic way for many of us, but practicing settling your heart and mind. Play some worship music and practice sitting quietly with the Lord.

Second-guessing is connected to People pleasing. I was second-guessing myself because I felt I had to make all the decisions, but I wasn't paying attention to the warning signs that came gently as a warning from the Holy

Spirit, not from me. Pay attention to the warning signs.

Some Things to Remember:

- Second-guessing yourself is not second-guessing yourself; if you are a Christian, you are second-guessing the leading of the Holy Spirit

- Repent and break that people-pleasing second-guessing spirit off you and keep doing it until it goes away. Break the agreement with people pleasing and second-guessing

- Second-guessing can have consequences; trust God instead!

- If there is too much noise, do not make any decisions until you are emotionally regulated or calm and can hear the Lord guiding you clearly; there is no confusion with the Lord.

- Feel comfortable saying "No." Real Talk Kim says, "No is a complete sentence," true story! Say no if you are being pressured; they will get over it. If they do not, they'll pout and give you the silent treatment, but that does not mean you did anything wrong. Stand strong.

"How it feels trying to fit in after you find out we are fighting principalities and powers and spiritual wickedness in high places."

Ephesians 6:12- "For we do not wrestle against flesh and blood, but against principalities, against powers, against the rulers of the darkness of this age, against spiritual hosts of wickedness in the heavenly places.

PART THREE

Conflict with Others:

Contending with People,
Places & Things

"When someone shows you who they are, believe them; the first time."- Maya Angelou

CHAPTER 9

Assess the Situation: Know your Enemy &

The Spirit Behind the Situation

The first step in problem-solving is assessing the problem. As a Christian in the workplace, to get right to the root of the issue, you will need to determine the spirit behind the personality, behavior, situation, or attack you are battling against. Yes, we're going there. The fact that you are reading this book means you

MONIKA T. MORRISSETTE, MSW, LCSW

are dealing with people, places, and things in
the workplace that have you stressed out. My
Workplace Bestie, you are battling evil. We
must discuss the reality of the world we live in.
Since we are Christians, it's not just pop culture
reasons, such as gaslighting or narcissistic
behavior. These terms have been widely used in
pop culture. As a Christ follower, we are going
a bit deeper. When you truly understand what is
behind the evil, it becomes a game-changer. It's
all about strategy. Satan is not creative; he uses
the same attack repeatedly. It has been said that
Satan overplays his hand. What you have been
experiencing at work is a pattern. It may involve
different circumstances and people, but the
same spirit behind it is trying to silence you,
bring you down, wear you out, and put you in

your place. Good news! You have what you need to overcome. 2 Peter 1:3 says, *"as his divine power has given to us all things that pertain to life and godliness, through the knowledge of him who called us by glory and virtue."*

Keep in mind this truth, as it says in Isaiah 54:17, *"No weapon formed against you shall prosper, and every tongue which rises against you in judgment, You shall condemn. This is the heritage of the servants of the Lord, and their righteousness is from Me," says the Lord."* You have heard it said the weapon will form, but it shall not prosper. Many weapons have been formed against me in the workplace; I'm certain you have also experienced spiritual warfare in the workplace.

Toxic workplaces are made up of mean-spirited people who have partnered with Satan and his demons with a demonic assignment to attack Christians. Toxic places are full of confusion, and I constantly felt power struggles with people who gave the appearance they were decent, only to operate in counterfeit kindness. They were full of witchcraft, consisting of controlling and manipulative behavior. Ruthless behavior in a toxic workplace is subtle and begins with jealousy, causing a toxic person to live offended and slander their target using gossip. Toxic people willfully decide to resist anything you do and say. They use their lying tongues and deceitful words to distort the truth, making themselves appear as victims to gain control and influence, while accusing you and telling lies to gain the upper hand. When you see the phony character of these individuals, and they know they cannot control you by their witchcraft, then you become the target. You will be rejected, talked about, and lied on. When they cannot control you, these toxic people become offended. Then they attack you with their lying tongues to malign your reputation, calling your character into question, and persuading others with their victimhood.

They feel and live rejected and offended, and are miserable, and they want you to feel that way too. These toxic people are very tormented. One of them even shared with me that she could not sleep at night and constantly had nightmares. I prayed for and with this person, really hoping she would be set free and have peace. The attacks increase when those demons in toxic people see that you are a Christian, even more so if you are a praying, faith-filled, Spirit-led Christian. The demonic stronghold operating in this former colleague caused her to continue to resist anything I said or did. Her torment and rejection made her a miserable person, and the only way to feel less weak was to try to control and manipulate external things to give her a sense of power and control. She was able to control the external things, but she could not control me. When you can't be manipulated or controlled or pushed around, you become the target.

Toxic workplaces are unsupportive if you refuse to drink the Kool-Aid. If you are not easily controlled and have standards, you will constantly be challenged. Toxic workplaces want conformity to their way only. When you are not a "yes person," you are not like them. There is always a point person in every organization and department who is the catalyst stirring up strife. If you are a leader in a toxic workplace, you likely receive no support, only resistance and rebellion. When a toxic workplace has put a target on your back, the disrespect is evident. Colleagues show contempt and resistance toward your leadership in every way possible, undermining your authority based on what they observed others doing and saying to you. Most likely, these individuals cannot think on their own. They are messy people anyway, who have listened to the perpetrator(s) of workplace toxicity.

Toxic workplaces cause a Christian doing their job to be the target of humiliation, which leads to dishonor, which breeds disrespect. Once that door is cracked open, harassing, hindering, and interfering spirits, including racism, run rampant. Toxic workplaces may give you a seat at the table, but they often attempt to set you up to fail by not preparing the table. Example: there are eight individuals, and there are only chairs and a place setting for 7. Toxic workplaces foster a culture of competition, pitting individuals against one another and pushing aside others. To get that seat, someone is always left out or never given the tools or support needed to lead, grow, or effectively contribute to the organization. It is usually the Christian who does not scheme or lie, and it leaves you feeling always left out, on the fringe, and never accepted. It left me feeling like everyone was working against me, not with me. I know God is for me, but I always felt in toxic workplaces that none of my colleagues were for me, and their behavior was evident.

Toxic workplaces are a breeding ground for repeated disrespect because they foster a culture of constant rejection, rebellion, and dishonor against anyone who challenges the toxic workplace's culture. Instead of unity, continuous resistance occurs when a person desires control and does not respect leadership and authority. The person resisting wants to be in control so badly that they attack the leader to avoid accountability, driven by pride, arrogance, and refusal to follow. People have their agendas in toxic workplaces. Just look at society, it's a problem that no one wants to respect authority. This is why this dynamic is increasingly a problem in the workplace. It is never easy to lead individuals who are rebellious, contrary, or disrespectful. Workplace bestie, let's not be people like this who cannot be led. In the workplace, we may work for toxic employers or organizations, but we ultimately work for God, the creator of Heaven and Earth. There is confusion, hindrances, and harassment of every kind. Toxic workplaces claim to be for the good of all but operate in racism and reverse discrimination. For that reason, toxic workplaces treat Christian leaders with contempt, leaving you feeling dismissed.

In the last few paragraphs, how many toxic workplace characteristics are familiar to you? Which ones are you struggling with? What have you experienced or witnessed others experiencing?

This scripture helped me to navigate toxic workplaces. Remember the Bible says, in Psalm 23, "*You prepare a table before me in the presence of my enemies; You anoint my head with oil; My cup runs over. Surely goodness and mercy shall follow you all the days of your life; And I will dwell in the house of the Lord, forever.*

Knowing the spirit behind people and interactions will help you understand what you are battling and reclaim the authority given to you by Father God as a child of God, as the daughter of the Most High God. Your prayers will be more specific when battling spiritual battles. Knowing the spirit behind a person reveals two key things: how you are being attacked and what issues that person has. For example, you may be interacting with a divisive person who gossips, is always contrary, and stirs up strife, yet never takes responsibility. This person is deflecting their insecurity onto others in an attempt to control situations outside their comfort zone. These individuals appear assertive and knowledgeable, but they lack humility and truth, and they attack you due to their insecurity. The enemy does not like the truth. Insecure people have bought into a lie, and their behavior follows suit. These individuals don't want their insecurity exposed, so they devise and scheme, working against you, the one whose compass points to truth. This type of person creates confusion, giving the appearance that you do not know what you are doing. Confronting this type of person causes them to then behave like a victim. They weaponize their tears or try to act innocently. It's a bait and switch with smoke and mirrors with them. They are so rooted in lies that they must wreak havoc to maintain their lie, and they scoped out the truthteller and put a bullseye on your back.

Yes, this sounds like a gas lighter and a narcissist. However, this is a weak person whom Satan and his demons are using to control and manipulate to get their way, wear you out, and move you out of the way. This is an example of a lying spirit, a controlling and manipulative spirit. If you are in Leadership and experiencing this, it is likely a manifestation of a Jezebel Spirit. The Jezebel spirit always goes after the leader. They want to be on top because they cannot be led, and they do not respect authority, so they go after the person in authority.

A Jezebel spirit must be the center of attention; they need the spotlight, and anyone threatening that need is attacked and taken out. How do you contend with this? First, you never battle this in your own strength; you must take authority in the name of Jesus. The name of Jesus and his shed Blood is where the power is! You do that in your prayer time. You remember the movie "*War Room*" well; that is where you go to battle by prayer. Knowing this will help you not respond out of offense but in the Spirit. Satan wants you to react in the flesh so he can use others to accuse you and point out your flaws to shut you down somehow. Maya Angelou is quoted as saying, "*When someone shows you who they are, believe them the first time.*" No matter the good you want to see in that person, do not be misled; be aware.

You can pray for them during your prayer time, asking God to heal and restore them. Praying for our enemies is being obedient to God's word. Now, let's be real: when someone behaves as our enemy, it is not a tea party. We must learn to spot this early on, so we are not reactive but proactive people. Proverbs 27:12 says, "*A prudent man foresees evil and hides himself, But the simple pass on and are punished."* When you see something, don't ignore it or pretend it will go away; evil will remain as long as it is tolerated. We do not confront in the flesh. We confront evil with the Holy Spirit, utilizing supernatural weapons such as prayer, taking authority in the name of Jesus, binding and loosing, pleading the Blood of Jesus, and not forgetting the Full Armor of God. You do not fight evil demonic spirits in your own strength.

Racism, yes, it's still a thing, but it is a demonic spirit rooted in pride, arrogance, division, and offense. I would be remiss if I did not address this as a black woman. I write not from a place of victimhood but calling it like I see it. I refuse to participate in victimhood, but

I will also not ignore this because, as a black woman, I have experienced people disrespecting, dishonoring, and second-guessing me because they did not think I was qualified or felt they needed to challenge me in some way all the time. I did not physically align with their preference or view of who a leader is.

There is nothing special about racism; it is a demonic spirit that is divisive and very toxic. We can even face this from people who look like us, and yes, anyone, any race, and even races that have historically been discriminated against are and can be very racist. You can have all the work experience and credentials, yet still face constant disrespect and be treated as if you're never good enough. I wore myself out trying to be the best, to be better when I was compared to others and to some who did not have my experience or my qualifications. I was fighting people, places, and things, and that's not how I want you to handle this. Hear me, racism exists, but it is not the cause; evil is the cause.

My thought is that using racism as your focus or crutch will only keep you focused on the person, place, and thing, and not who you are, and more importantly, whose you are. A person can be racist because of their thinking, behavior, and beliefs. I had a supervisor who thought it would be funny to refer to me as an "ABW." This person was being a racist. They knew fully what they were saying. The Holy Spirit told me what those letters meant, and then this person confirmed it out of their mouth. If you don't know, ABW stands for "Angry Black Woman. This was so out of line and uncalled for. I told her, "Don't ever refer to me in that manner again." This person laughed and did it again on another occasion. Because crazy folks need to hear it one more time for it to sink in, I again told her, "Never tell me that again." Something must have woken her up out of her ignorance LOL! She never did that to my face again. Was this frustrating and insulting? Yes.

Were this person's ignorant words going to keep me from succeeding? No. So we confront the hindering spirit and keep it moving! Seeing racism as nothing more than a demonic hindering spirit, well, that is the solution. We know what to do with a hindering spirit. We use the authority given to us by the blood of Jesus! When racism impacts people, it's a hindering spirit. So, you handle it the way you would handle any other demonic spirit, take authority over it in the name of Jesus, and plead the Blood of Jesus. Praying and declaring that the enemy's plot and plan would be exposed was a daily prayer of mine. You handle this by seeking God.

God is the great I AM and the "Great Equalizer." I decided to see God as bigger than the bigots. Because He is my provider and knows all and sees all, I trust God and put my life in His hands. I spoke scripture and declared I can do all things through Christ who strengthens me! I refuse to be anyone's victim. Yes, there is racism, but we as Christians must handle this differently than how our society handles it. How, by taking authority over racism and renouncing racism's presence in your workplace and pleading the Blood of Jesus. I have seen God maneuver things and work things out on my behalf; there is nothing too hard for God.

God knows what you are up against; this has not caught God by surprise! God knows the intentions and motives of man's heart, and he will not leave you in this place. He will help you truly overcome. You have to decide NOT to come into agreement that racism is controlling your destiny. This may not be a popular truth, but as your Workplace bestie, I'm here to tell you the truth. Refuse to give the enemy or any human being that kind of control over you.

As a Christian, my life is in God's hands. It says in Revelation 12:11, "*And they overcame him by the blood of the lamb and the word of their testimony,* and they loved not their lives unto the death." Choose to believe the truth in God's word. I am an overcomer by the blood of the lamb and by the word of my testimony, and you are too. It takes a shift in your mindset about this issue. You are no victim, you are a victor, and nothing can hinder you. If you are not a person of color, you can also take authority over racism in your workplace. There are instances of reverse discrimination as well. Either way, it's wrong; racism is a divisive tool of the enemy used to create confusion and hinder unity. Two wrongs do not make a right.

All this discussion about people, places, and things: remember this when contending with others. You are not fighting people. As it says in Ephesians 6:12, "*For we wrestle not against flesh and blood, but against principalities, against powers, against the rulers of the darkness of this world, against spiritual wickedness in high places.*" When you identify relationship patterns you have experienced, typical interactions with others, or things that always seem to trip you up, write them down in your journal and seek God in prayer about them. The counselor in me would ask you to examine the situation and issues you've identified, along with your thoughts and emotions, and how those patterns and reactions have influenced your actions. Looking deeper at this will give you insight and self-awareness to get to the root of the issues that keep repeating, and it is uncomfortable. Praise God, he does not leave us there in the mess. Decide to seek what God says and has given you to get through and overcome. There is hope, and it starts with what God says in his word. Luke 10:19 says, *"Behold, I give you the authority to trample on serpents and scorpions, and over all the power of the enemy, and nothing shall by any means hurt you."* The keyword here is "authority," defined in Vine's Expository Dictionary of the New Testament Words as:

Authority (from the impersonal verb exesti, "it is lawful"). Meaning to "leave or permission," or liberty of doing as one pleases, it passed to that of "the ability or strength with which one is endued," then to that of the

"power of authority," the right to exercise power or "the

power of rule or government," the power of one whose

will and commands must be obeyed by others.

When you have had workplace issues, you almost begin to accept it as "it is what it is." Not so, you have been freed by the finished work of the cross, the death, burial, and resurrection of Jesus. You no longer live in darkness, bondage, or live a life of "it is what it is." You are not defeated. Let me encourage you to read and re-read Luke 10:19 until it resonates with you. Speak that scripture over your situation. You have been given authority. What does this mean? When you are attacked and kicked down, you use your authority in battle—the sword of the Spirit, which is the word of God. You speak with authority over the situation. You do not do this in your power; you do this in the name of Jesus, by the Blood of Jesus. Every demon must flee at the name of Jesus. Evil cannot exist where there is light and where the Blood of Jesus is. To contend with people, places, and things, recognize your authority and use it by speaking the word of God and pleading the Blood of Jesus over yourself, your workplace, and all your interactions. The enemy cannot cross a line where the Blood of Jesus has been drawn.

Some Things to Remember:

When you know, you know, and knowing
is half the battle! - G. I. Joe

- Assess your situation or patterns

- Identify what you are battling and the spirit behind it

- Remember you are not fighting flesh and blood but the evil principalities in this world

- Seek Father God for wisdom and strategy

- Be aware: how do these people, places, and things cause you to think, feel, and behave

- What have you believed about yourself or the situation? Are there any lies? What is true

- Do not fight battles using your own strength; use your supernatural weapons

- Put on the Full Armor of God

- Take Authority using the Word of God and Plead the Blood of Jesus

- You are not a victim, you are a victor

"Mean Girls Rarely Grow Up...

*The High School hallways have now become the break
room at work!"*

CHAPTER 10

Gossips, Busybodies, & Mean Girls, Oh My!

Let's call them nice nasty. Smile in your face, stab you in your back, and still smile in your face, again, while behaving like a victim, crying and talking out of both sides of their mouth. These are the same folks who, when you need to speak the truth to them as a leader or give them feedback, would weaponize their tears and cry and behave like a victim. People nowadays have a problem hearing the truth. They crumble and cry like you did something to them. Then they try to assassinate your character by gossiping about you. That's a mouthful. People do not know why they dislike you. You will know if you've never really spoken to someone and they have an attitude towards you; it's likely because they have been part of conversations where you were talked about negatively. People can be ridiculous; they give themselves away. People who were rude and nasty were convinced they disliked me because someone else didn't like me. Most likely, it was because I wouldn't let them push me around, or the truth was more than they could handle, so they went with what they thought they knew about me, which was nothing.

Silly human beings, unfortunately, silly women. We have to be better than this. In some places, I never fit in at work because I wouldn't gossip about others, so I'd either leave or interrupt to stop the person who was starting to gossip. You do not need to know someone else's information about another person. It is nothing but gossip. If you sit quietly and listen to gossip, even if you are saying nothing, you are complicitly participating and silently agreeing with it. Workplace Bestie, this is a huge warning flag I'm waving. Separate yourself from being a party to maligning someone else's character and reputation. What will stop anyone is if you tell them. Hey, when I meet them, may I share with them what you told me. Just know, when you are not a gossip, you cannot be controlled or swayed by others, so it makes you a target, and you will not be "one of the girls." Who wants to be part of the mean girl brigade, really? Not me and not you!

I was a resident assistant back in college, and oh boy, did I learn quickly how rotten grown women can be. I was selected in my third year in college to serve in this capacity. It was fun and for the most part I enjoyed living in the dorms/residence halls, but…I was the resident assistant for the all-female dorm. My job was to lead and manage that dorm. Let me repeat, I was the resident assistant for the all-female dorm. What a learning experience. I learned how unsupportive, entitled, and mean grown women can be. These were women, mostly young adults around my age, give or take a few years, and some old enough to know better and do better, but chose to fully engage in nonsense and foolishness.

I was excited about this and wanted to make a difference. I planned all summer, used my own money from a summer job to purchase and make individual welcome greetings for each resident. I made my decorations and tried to make everyone feel welcome. You know how people get when you do too much; they don't appreciate it. They take it for granted and feel entitled. I did what I could and tried my best. Well, I cannot believe how miserable women can be toward one another. They were quite rebellious, rude, and disrespectful. I was a people pleaser, and it's clearer what personality this attracts. As we have learned, it attracts rebellious, controlling, and insecure individuals, who seek to attack and cause drama. What should you learn from this example? Identify your issues, and you will identify the evil spirit that is attracted to what you are struggling with. That's where you will be attacked. Some of these dorm girls were jealous because they thought they owned me and that, somehow, being a resident assistant meant I couldn't have a life outside of this role. I was too available until I was not, and they just about lost their minds. So many of them had a problem with me having a boyfriend, and to be truthful, they were miserable and jealous. It was unreal, some of the wildest stuff I had seen as a college student in the dorms. The accusations, lies, and complaints. It was so bad that they decided to meet with the residence hall director to complain. A funny thing happened after that; several people came to my room to apologize, saying they hadn't meant for the meeting to turn into a character assassination. But it was the start of issues in the workplace settings for me.

Mean girls and more mean girls. Workplace Bestie, some of them never quite grow up. I have constantly been challenged when in leadership positions. Being in leadership roles in the church has also brought some similar dynamics. The demonic spirit in those people who attack others is attracted to the brokenness in another person, for example, people pleasing, a fear and cowering spirit, timidity, and fear of man. They gravitate to others whom they can attack. A person who is controlling, manipulative, and who has a lying tongue is operating in witchcraft. They are attracted to a person who has a cowering spirit, one who is a people pleaser, a perfectionist, because this is how they get away with abusing and tormenting someone. It boils down to their need to control people, places, and things that makes them feel powerful.

The people pleaser will always blame themselves. Do you struggle with perfectionism, second-guessing yourself, or timidity? Your reading this book is proof that God is not going to leave you in this place of despair and frustration. I pray for the same deliverance I received for you. As Christ followers, we will inevitably contend with darkness on this side of Heaven. But we have weapons for our warfare, and they will tear down strongholds and the evil, causing some of your colleagues to operate in witchcraft. Witchcraft is an attempt to control someone. You will find that if you have already assessed the patterns in your life, you will recognize the ones you keep encountering. Different places and different faces, same attitudes and personalities.

We may never be part of the crew, never quite accepted; one person may not like you, or there may be a group against you. Cliques of women can be nasty and just downright mean. Funny things about worldly women, they never want to support you. They seem to want to do things their way. They have their ideas and attempt to undermine, undercut, and interfere, trying to create division and drama. There is so much competition between women that a constant "one-up game" is always being played. It's the queen bee syndrome that turns a professional setting into schoolyard drama and a reality television show - just a hot mess of nonsense and foolishness. Workplace Bestie, mean girls are jealous girls who want to take your glow and shine by knocking your crown off your head. You have the light of Jesus in you; nothing can take that.

Some Things to Remember:

- Mean girls are jealous and insecure girls-
  pray for them, they are clueless

- Now, don't you be a mean girl! If you are a gossip girl, drop that nonsense and foolishness now! Repent and separate yourself from the mean girl brigade!

- Let them gossip about you, let them talk, you know the truth.

- I love what I've heard Real Talk Kim say, of those who behave like your enemies, "they are just confused fans!"

"I'm sorry," says the Silent Partners while also saying:
"Not my circus, not my monkeys"- Polish Proverb

CHAPTER 11

Silent Partners:

Don't Be One

These are the ones who are one way

with you, another way in public, and yet

another way with executive leadership. They

have witnessed your mistreatment and did

nothing about it; they stayed silent and watched.

It's funny that I worked in the social work

profession my entire career, and 99% of social

workers watched harmful things happen in front of them and did nothing. Many of them entered this profession to help alleviate the pain and suffering of others, yet they were complicit in causing pain and suffering in the workplace. But Silent Partners remain silent. They smile and are exceptionally kind, but lack backbone due to their fear of their own job loss. I suppose of their own job loss. The social work profession has long been known to be in the trenches, fighting for those who have no voice, challenging what is wrong, and championing change to improve things for others. However, many still stay silent and watch their colleagues endure harm. Silent partners are useless. Yes, that is harsh, but it's the truth. I have been the recipient of this pansy behavior disguised as concern—people who smile in your face only not to have your back. Let's face it, they are people too, and they are fearful.

Workplace Bestie, put on your seatbelt; this next part is going to be a bumpy ride. But lean in, I will share with you how Silent Partners are no help. I recall my first year in a leadership position, when the CEO didn't like me. Why didn't this human being like me? I often refer to the evil people, mean people, and ridiculous people as "human beings." It helps me remember they, too, are made in the image of God. I want to remember that they are a person who needs to be prayed for. Well, I stood my ground for a moment on an issue I wasn't comfortable with and communicated it professionally. This person was new to the organization and town, and most likely wanted everyone to like them. I spy a clue about insecurity. Did you pick that up in the description of this human being's behavior? This individual developed various strategies to gain the approval of others and establish a position for himself within the organization and business sector. From what has been discussed thus far in this book, do you see control and manipulation?

Well, when you push back on a fragile person and speak the truth or have a differing opinion, you are punished and taught a lesson. I was gossiped about, multiple attempts to pressure me, fear tactics used to cause me to fear my job being taken from me, all because I professionally disagreed. And because this leader was disappointed with me and because I did not just do what he wanted without question, he decided to humiliate me and dishonor me publicly in front of people I was tasked to lead. My direct supervisor at the time also sat there complicit in this debacle. This person claimed to be a Christian, but their actions did not reflect it. This one act set the tone for the people I was tasked to lead. It let them know that speaking up was not safe, that they shouldn't align with Monika, or they could suffer the same fate. The message was essentially that they should only align with those they like, which is code for not showing public support or loyalty to Monika. Silent Partners are one way in public and another way in private. This was fake. I admit this was so disgusting to me that I had to check my own attitude many times. It was hard to love people who behaved like counterfeits. People did not respect me and were not loyal to me because, in their minds, that would be a nail in their coffin professionally. Workplace Bestie, I needed a strong Christian colleague who wasn't afraid to speak the truth and have my back.

So, when they witnessed the CEO disrespect, dishonor, and humiliate me during my staff meeting, they sat in silence. I mean, zero people spoke up on my behalf. It hurt so bad, and I had to learn to heal from this wound because it impacted how I interacted with other colleagues, employees, and leaders. This so-called leader spoke negatively of me, saying I was not a good leader, and pointed out what they felt I was lacking. They verbalized publicly that they had to find someone else for a role they were creating, all in front of those I was tasked to lead. My team did not have my back. No one spoke up for me; they all sat there and said nothing until after the meeting. The funny thing is, after the meeting where this happened, several people said, "Oh, you didn't deserve that." The bleeding hearts showed up and tried to tend to me. No, I did not stick around to help them feel better. I looked everyone in the eye during that meeting and watched the disgusting silence. I have publicly stood up for people and spoken the truth, but it was not extended to me. Those who never spoke up have no idea that they were among the people executive leadership was considering firing. I spoke up for some of them to preserve their jobs. That was a difficult season. I had to decide what I was going to believe about myself, or would I accept the lie and the attack perpetrated. I fought on, but struggled with resisting the lies others said about me. But when new people come on board, it doesn't take them long to catch on as well. They see how you are treated; they hear the gossip that was done to ruin your reputation, and those people also sit silent. Silent people disappoint me because their silence represents a significant issue within the workplace.

Every Jezebel needs an Ahab. Silent people are the Ahab's in this story, allowing the spirit of Jezebel to have full reign and destroy. They picked a side, and for many of them, things went well while they sat back and witnessed the mistreatment of those who told the truth and spoke up. While we can empathize with their need to stay safe, fear does not look good on anyone. I have had to forgive those individuals. Things went well for them on the job; they got in step with the Jezebels and partnered with them. The silent folks, well, you have to make a conscious decision to stay silent, which means you have thought this through in your rational mind and still decided to partner with lies by not speaking the truth. I'll park that there.

Yes, Workplace Bestie, it still stings, but thank God I am on the other side of this. God helped me through. I forgive the silent partners and the perpetrators, but I ask God daily to help me forgive these folks. I choose to release them, lay them at the feet of Jesus, and forgive them by faith. I am not a fan of Silent Partners. I pray God helps you to see these people as he sees them. What I learned: let me make sure to look at any area where I have been silent and repent of that. When this happens, you know who is real, who is phony, who is nice/nasty, and who is a counterfeit in your life. Sometimes it hurts, but as Maya Angelou is quoted as essentially saying, believe people when they show you who they are. People can smile, but that does not always mean they have your best interests at heart. Look at the behavior, does it match what they say, does it match what they say in private with you? Is that person different, or do they stay the same, or behave differently when others are around, or when leadership is around? Fake people will morph into whatever allows them to maintain themselves. Don't be a Silent Partner; you are acting out of fear. Toxic workplaces continue because of the layers of fear that toxic leaders perpetuate. In Mathew 18:20, it says, *"For where two or three are gathered together in My name, I am there in the midst of them."* The Bible also says in Ecclesiastes 4:12, *"Though one may be overpowered by another, two can withstand him. And a threefold cord is not quickly broken."*

Some Things to Remember:

- Never sit back and watch others get humiliated in public

- A leader who participates in humiliation, dishonor, and disrespect is no leader

- When you are not comfortable with something, pray about it, stand firm, ask God what to do, and do it.

- Believe what is true about you, cancel the attack on your character in the name of Jesus.

- Plead the Blood of Jesus over your soul for the wounds that brought you harm in the workplace.

"Real anointing irritates

real demons.

That's why some people

can't stand you &

they don't even know why

They are possessed.

It's not personal.

It's spiritual".

-Author Unknown-

Parable of the Wheat and the Tares

Matthew 13:24-30

CHAPTER 12

But they are supposed to be Christians!

The Wheat & The Tares

If it acts like a duck and quacks like a duck, well, it is a duck! The Bible talks about the Wheat and the Tares. You will learn, if you have not already, that there are so many people who say they are a Christian with the words they use. You have some who will say they attend church and give the impression that they are a "Christian." However, their behavior, words, and attitude suggest otherwise. Then you have others who use flowery words and Cheshire-cat-like smiles that make them seem holier than thou… Well, watch that one; they look like they are everyone's answer, and all they do is create destruction. There is a trail of it around them. The Bible says in Matthew 7:20, "Therefore by their fruits you will know them." And if you see fruit, watch out for what that fruit looks like or smells like. You will know that what looks good is not always good. It may look shiny and new and prim and proper on the outside, but it is death and destruction dressed up. You can't put lipstick on a pig and call it something else; it's still a pig, but now

with obnoxious red lips!

The Parable of the Wheat and the Tares

is mentioned in the Bible in Matthew 13:24-30

as follows:

> *Another parable He put forth to them, saying: "The kingdom of heaven is like a man who sowed good seed in his field;*
>
> *"but while men slept, his enemy came and sowed Tares among the Wheat and went his way.*
>
> *"But when the grain had sprouted and produced a crop, then the Tares also appeared.*
>
> *"So the servants of the owner came and said to him, 'Sir, did you not sow good seed in your field? How then does it have Tares?'*
>
> *"He said to them, 'An enemy has done this.' The servants said to him, 'Do you want us then to go and gather them up?'*
>
> *"But he said, 'No, lest while you gather up the Tares you also uproot the Wheat with them.*
>
> *Let both grow together until the harvest, and at the time of harvest I will say to the reapers, "First gather together the Tares and bind them*

in bundles to burn them, but gather the Wheat into my barn.' "

I share this example of the Wheat and the Tares because not everyone who says they are a Christian is truly a surrendered follower of Jesus Christ. They may be so deceived that they do not realize their behavior tells something much worse about who they really are, who they are aligned with, and who they are really serving. I call them "counterfeits. The Bible says in 2 Corinthians 11:13-14,

> *"For such are false apostles, deceitful workers, transforming themselves into apostles of Christ. And no wonder! For Satan himself transforms himself into an angel of light."*

It boils down to this: Christians are bought and paid for, and their lives covered by the Blood of Jesus. When I refer to Counterfeits, I am speaking of those who have not surrendered their lives to Jesus. Those who live an unrepentant life, seeking their own way, cause destruction. I am not referring to Christians who are continuing to work out their Salvation and make errors at times. Romans 3:23 says, "for all have sinned and fall short of the glory of God." The difference between the Christians (Wheat) and the Counterfeits (Tares) is that the Wheat is repentant, surrenders, and has a holy conviction when they fall short because of the Holy Spirit in them. The Tares do not have any conviction and are not repentant; they are workers of iniquity and destruction and seek to divide, destroy, steal, and create confusion and disorder... sounds like Satan.

Those who call themselves "Christians" who are only counterfeits are partners with darkness and are being used by the enemy, Satan, and his demons. Have you asked yourself why other "Christians" are not experiencing gossip and toxic workplace culture and bullying behavior? Why does this seem to be happening to me? If you are like me, you wonder why you are on the receiving end of so many attacks. My mission was to go to work and do good work. I minded my own business and focused on what was set before me. Workplace Bestie, I'm certain this describes you, too. The answer to this question is that darkness always partners with darkness, covering it and protecting its own. When there is light from a Christian, darkness will always join forces to eliminate it. The Wheat symbolizes true Believers, Christians. The Tares symbolize, in my opinion, the counterfeits who call themselves Christians. The counterfeits look like and even sound like genuine Christians…but they are not. As my mentor, Charlana, would say about people, places, and things, "Be careful about what seems right and sounds right."

I have read and heard about the Parable of the Wheat and the Tares many times in church and in devotionals. It's a warning for us to be aware of how evil can penetrate good things, good places, even churches, and workplaces that Christians oversee. I am no farmer; I am a city girl from the Inland Empire in California. My father's side of the family were farmers. It makes me laugh to think that I, this city girl, took Agriculture Science in high school, and well, I'll park that vision there! But if you are not a farmer like me but want to be, that's okay; the Holy Spirit will help you spot the Tares. My hope is that you listen...truly listen to the Holy Spirit as He shows you the Tares among you.

I learned that the way to know the difference between Wheat and the Tares is when the time of harvest comes, the Wheat dies to itself and its head is bowed. What does that look like? It looks like true humility, love, sacrifice, not seeking or demanding their own way, and certainly not drawing attention to themselves. The Tares, on the other hand, stick straight up. Why? There is nothing in them. They are hollow shells that will blow away when the Wheat is gathered at harvest time. They stick straight up when gathered among the Wheat, so they are noticeable; they are not humble but full of pride and arrogance. They look the part and even sound the part, but toxic workplaces protect them because they are really not Christians. Remember, darkness aligns with and protects other sources of darkness. They are counterfeits.

People become Christians because they have confessed that they are sinners who need a Savior, repented of their sins, asked for forgiveness, and confessed with their mouths that Jesus Christ is their Lord and Savior; they are saved, and the Holy Spirit comes into their hearts to dwell. The counterfeits, on the other hand, will warm the pews/seats of churches and believe that they are "good people" and are on their way to heaven…because they are "so good". This is a huge deception. The Tares do not have the Holy Spirit in them.

In Romans 8:16, the Scripture says, "The Spirit Himself bears witness with our spirit that we are children of God". I met a random lady I didn't know at the grocery store. I turned the corner with my shopping cart at the same time this sweet older lady did. She greeted me, "Hello, my sister, I know you." I smiled at her. She stopped and said I know you are my sister! I have never met this sweet lady, but I immediately knew she was a sister in

Christ—a Christian—from the way she greeted

me. That confirmation resonated in my spirit. I

will not forget that. My mentor, Charlana,

always discusses and warns about being aware

of that check in your spirit. As I have discussed

in this book, the time I did not pay close

attention to that check, and things became a hot

mess after that. I did not have a check in my

spirit about this lady; I had confirmation she

was a sister in Christ! In the grocery store, I

hugged this woman I had never met, and I

cannot tell you how blessed I felt. One that she

recognized me to be a sister in Christ, all glory

to God, as it was not me, it was the light of

Jesus! During a time I felt so hurt by others,

God allowed me to experience the confirmation

of the Holy Spirit in someone I had never met.

This was a golden experience! That was what I called a divine appointment. I left that woman's presence feeling encouraged and uplifted. I really cannot explain it, so I give glory and honor to God! The Bible says we will entertain angels, and you know I strongly believe God ordered that woman's steps because God knew I needed a touch of encouragement from the Lord!

People who are Tares leave destruction in their wake, and they are exhausting to be around. Their only purpose is to wear out the Saints of God. They do not refresh, but they are in the way, preventing everyone from being refreshed or recharged. There is always, I repeat always, confusion with them. Regardless of their title or experience, they may appear so great, but…Tares have toxic ambition and

control issues. I have a name from them,

"Educated Annoyances." A person who is a

tare has made it their entire purpose and

mission to cause confusion and destruction so

they can stand straight up and say, "Look at me,

I'm on top". They are selfish, and because they

do not have the Holy Spirit in them, they are

unable to be convicted of wrong behavior, such

as being unable to follow and come under those

in authority, so that order is maintained. They

challenge order and create confusion. Wheat

bows their head because they are full of the

Holy Spirit and are humble. Tares are full of

nothing. So their fruit is nothing. Like a

decorative bowl of wax fruit that seems right,

looks good and shiny, you can't eat it because it's toxic to your health.

Another way to identify Tares is found in another passage in the Bible, from Proverbs 6:12-19, which says:

A worthless person, a wicked man, walks with a perverse mouth; He winks with his eyes, He shuffles his feet, He points with his fingers; Perversity is in his heart, He devises evil continually, He sows discord. Therefore, his calamity shall come suddenly; Suddenly he shall be broken without remedy. These six things the LORD hates, yes, seven are an abomination to Him: A proud look, A lying tongue, Hands that shed innocent blood, A heart that devises wicked plans, Feet that are swift in running to evil, A false witness who speaks lies, And one who sows discord among brethren.

Tares never stand for truth. Well, they stand for "their truth," which is still built on a lie. Tares lie to maintain their counterfeit façade. Tares are swift to lie, cause confusion, and bring calamity. They do not like order, surrender, or authority. They are disruptive. They make everything about themselves and focus attention on themselves. Again, there is no real edible or nurturing fruit. They are proud and arrogant, never humbling themselves. They challenge order and authority because they are unruly and believe they know better.

Tares can never give anything at Harvest time. Harvest time is when the real work happens; it's the time for gathering. There is nothing in or to the Tares, and when Harvest time comes, they will be unable to do anything

211

because they have nothing. The Bible says they will be burned up because what they have is not fit for use in the Kingdom of God. Scheming, controlling, lying, manipulation, etc., are works of darkness and are of no use in the Kingdom of God. On the other hand, humility, surrender, truth, love, peace, etc., are some of the good fruits of the Holy Spirit. I actually feel sad for someone who has nothing. It's pitiful. As much as the Tares disgust our flesh, Workplace Bestie, we are called to pray for our enemies. We can separate from them, mark them as counterfeits, but still pray they will come to the saving grace of Jesus. God does not want anyone to perish, and neither should we.

Some Things to Remember

- Put the Full armor of God on, and pray and declare scripture, don't go half-dressed to the battle

- Ask the Lord to give you discernment to identify the Wheat & the Tares

- Identify the spirit behind the people, places, and things

- Identify what you have been tolerating, repent, and take back your authority with your words

- Pray about how God wants you to proceed, pray for strategy, and the Holy Spirit will show you

- Plead the blood of Jesus over your workplace

- Put your trust in the Lord

- Cover everything in prayer, before every conversation, interaction, meeting, anything. Don't give up any territory to the enemy.

- Watch and pray, when you feel pressure or observe behavior or experience an attack, deal with it in the moment. Excuse yourself to the ladies' room for privacy to address whatever comes up.

- Do not feel pressured to respond until you have sought the Lord; you don't have to mention this to anyone.

- Assess where you are triggered and deal with conflicts with yourself that are open doors to the enemy.

- The Tares were sent to disrupt the Wheat, but remember, Tares have nothing to give or contribute; they are really in the way of kingdom work. Tares are counterfeits; they seem right and sound right and may even look good on paper. When the real work comes, they become divisive and confused, seeking destruction.

- Remember lipstick on a pig does not change that the pig is still a pig!

PART FOUR

Exodus Prep:

Collect your Peace & See

your way outta there!

"It's not personal, it's just business!"
– from The Godfather

"You've got to know

when to hold 'em

Know when to fold 'em

Know when to walk away

And know when to run

You never count your money

When you're sittin' at the table

There'll be time

enough for counting

When the dealin's done"

- The Gambler -

by Kenny Rogers

CHAPTER 13

Bloom Where You're planted, But Don't Get too Comfortable

Wherever you are, ensure that you are continually growing and developing; do not let yourselves become stagnant and irrelevant. In the Bible, it is written that we are to stir up the gifts that have been given to us. Each of you has gifts and talents. When you are in a toxic workplace, working around unhealed, immature, and insecure human beings who have a title and some without the fancy titles but who have been given some pseudo authority that allows for toxic cultures and workplaces, well, don't allow yourselves to stop growing in response to the stress these people and situations are causing. You will have to rise above. When you see a problem, don't just jump ship; make sure you leave better than you came. Yes, leave things better than you found them, but you should leave better than you came. Make sure you use time to better yourself and prepare yourself for the next season.

You are probably wondering, "What is the next season?" If you spend time with God, as previously mentioned in this book, you will receive daily downloads from the Holy Spirit. If you struggle in this area, it's not too late. Spend time with the Lord over the weekend, and God will show up. Turn off social media, news, and distractions fast and pray to hear what the Lord would have you do; he will tell you the next step. Now you may not get the whole picture, but that is where trusting God and having faith come in.

Perhaps you have had some things come to your heart over the year, maybe something that has stirred an interest. That may be just the thing that the Lord wants you to step out into. Many times, we hesitate out of fear, or when you work in a toxic, abusive workplace, you are so beaten down by how you have been treated, you cannot see a way. This is one of the reasons I wrote this book. What I went through in a couple of different workplaces was disgraceful, but God has not wasted any of it. Maybe you haven't gone through the crushing, perhaps you have, or maybe you find yourself at your wits' end, or possibly you have even given up and picked this book up as a last-ditch effort before doing something drastic. I want to encourage you right now. I felt all the feels you could feel, experiencing the harm and just how evil people could be. First, remember you are not battling people; it is the wicked and the demonic that is working through people, it is the prince spirits of this world, it is not flesh and blood. It is very difficult to separate the two and see the person as a human being.

They give the appearance of so much power, but think for a minute just how weak, pathetic, and fragile someone must be to allow a demon to inhabit them. Pause there. You are not battling flesh and blood. If you were the person attacking, resisting, and fighting, you would have already won before they opened their mouth. This is supernatural… but don't let that scare you. As a child of God, the daughter of the Most High God, you have supernatural power. You have resurrection power. The same power that raised Jesus from the dead is in you.

We forget that when we are going through stress, and when we are at capacity with stress, strain, and people. I would say I do not have the bandwidth for this right now. In my strength, I do not. I worried about whether this was going to kill me, and I worried about the stress. I would have chest pain, palpitations, and if you are, please get checked out by a doctor who will get to the root of the problem. Remember, no band-aids, we want resolutions.

A word about getting comfortable: Bloom where you are planted, prepare, and avoid becoming too comfortable. When you get too comfortable, you miss warning signs because you stop looking. Never get comfortable. Comfort causes you to get haughty, arrogant, and prideful. You don't see things coming. I never got comfortable, possibly because I never felt at ease. While this was uncomfortable, it was necessary. Here is a brief example. I had horrible leaders I reported to in a couple of organizations I worked for. Please understand that among the places I worked, I had the blessing of excellent workplace managers/supervisors who were true leaders: Debbie, Sally, Susana, Angie, and Karen. I say that so they are separated from the abusive leaders who wounded me. Well, with changes in organizations and restructuring, the whole organization can be in chaos, positions shift, and people just lose their common decency, courtesy, and sense.

Gone are the days when working for an organization meant that your loyalty, dedication, and years of service were valued. Also, some organizations, under the guise of streamlining and restructuring, get rid of someone who was there for over 20 years, showing the utmost dishonor and disrespect with the canned comment, "Thank you for your years of service to the organization." So, I prayed about this, and God revealed this to me. That leader, with over 20 years of service to this organization, got comfortable. She was a whole lot better supervisor than what I had at the organization. While serving under her, I could breathe a bit better. Looking back, there were some things that I realized even about this kind supervisor.

There is a pride and false sense of security that comes. We need to learn to see the writing on the wall. Changes and shake-ups always mean that the crushing is about to happen. I learned about olive trees and how to pick olives. The tree is shaken, the olives are gathered, and then they are pressed and crushed. This is why we need to ensure our fruit is good, that we have good fruit to produce godly oil in us. If we do not have Jesus, we will have nothing but crushed olives and no oil. We survive the crushing because of the anointing of the Holy Spirit, but Jesus was crushed on the cross. He defeated death, hell, and the grave and rose again. So just like that old song, because he lives, I can face tomorrow. In 2 Corinthians 4:8-10, it says, *"we are hard pressed on every side, but not crushed; perplexed, but not in despair; persecuted, but not abandoned; struck down, but not destroyed. We always carry around in our body the death of Jesus, so that the life of Jesus may also be revealed in our body."* Another verse in Psalm 27:13-14 says, *"I had fainted, unless I had believed to see the goodness of the Lord in the land of the living. Wait on the Lord: be of good courage, and he shall strengthen thine heart: wait, I say, on the Lord."*

God is still good, but getting comfortable looks like feeling you have arrived. If you have not been crushed, but you are seeing it around you with others, just know that if you are a Christian living for Jesus, the crushing is coming for you, too. That is not to scare you, but promotion comes from God, and if you don't go through this, you will never know what is in you that either needs to get refined, purified, or rooted out. You will not be alone.

We have to decide whether we will be comfortable and useless, or experience a moment of discomfort that God will use to set others free for his Kingdom and his purpose. It's hard; surrender is hard.

Growing comfortable seems to mean no longer developing yourself to stay marketable. It means you have outgrown the organization, especially if it's a toxic workplace. The Bible says to stir up your gifts. Consider that you may need more training and learning to grow in what God has gifted you to do.

There is nothing bad about getting an education, certification, or training. Remember to be set apart first by the witness of Jesus in your life, and make sure you are prepared for what you will work on. We work in man's system, and man's system has rules and regulations. You may need a license, a master's degree, or additional certifications. But be working on this so you leave with something that will position you. The goal is not to stay in a toxic workplace; you want to move on to a better workplace, and your loyalty will be valued at the next place. But we leave when God says leave, we do not leave just to avoid. To grow, there are things you will have to go through and weather the storm. You will be viewed as a person with staying power; an organization that cannot retain people and maintain longevity has a systemic problem, and the character and integrity of those leading it are in question. Do not be lulled by comfort; it's false and a subtle way of taking you out when you least expect it. It's a rude awakening waiting to happen, and when it does, you're left in shock and disbelief, forced to react.

I came to the one organization as an MSW, worked, and in a down moment, I had a sweet neighbor who had a little dog like I do, and we connected over our little dogs. Well, she blessed me when I was out of work for a season and encouraged me to get back up and keep working to earn my license. No shame here, I eventually passed that exam and was licensed with the grace of God on top of grace on top of grace! I was rehired by a prior employer, this time as a Licensed Clinical Social Worker. While there, I earned a Qualified Supervisor credential to supervise clinical hours. Which came in handy when the long-time social work leader retired. I was then tapped to fill that role… but that was when the disrespect that was already there became even worse, right there.

So, I was so focused on work for a bit, I had no time and energy to prepare or get the certifications I was seeking. This is what I am talking about: the job, people, and the devil will use things, people, and situations to distract you and wear you out. This is where you must fight the fight of faith and ensure you look out for yourself, seeking the Lord's direction for you. You may not need any additional education. Make sure you keep a record of your wins, losses, and how you learned, as well as what you would do differently. You will need this when you interview. Secure letters of recommendation from those you trust. If you feel any inclination to leave, develop an exit strategy, and by all means, keep that to yourself. It's time to be in stealth mode, like B-2 stealth mode; no one will or should see your resignation coming. Know when to speak and when to stay quiet —that's a whole other lesson for another day and another time.

Some Things to Remember:

- Pray for a date from the Lord of when you should be leaving, keep that to yourself unless you have a mentor whom you can share with to pray with you.

- When you have that date, begin to make a timeline and plan, and keep that to yourself

- Before you give your notice, make sure all your pertinent and personal things are out of your office.

- Keep your business to yourself, keep it between you and God, and a trusted

mentor, and pray for strategy, the Holy
Spirit will give that to you!

- Make sure that on the day you submit
  your letter of resignation, you are
  prepared to exit that day or at any time.
  Some employers are nasty and evil like
  that. I'm warning you it's a trend now.
  Don't be surprised by anything. I put
  my work bag in my car because my
  office was already cleaned out. The only
  thing I took with me was the toilet
  paper I purchased with my own money
  for the restroom I used.

- Take your preparation little by little:
  slow and steady wins the race!

- Clean your office or cubicle; do not
  leave it a mess. You are a daughter of

the Most High God. You have class;

even when others do you wrong, you do

better. Go higher, remember Eagles do

not fly with Crows.

"Congratulations on quitting your job without being escorted out of the building!"

CHAPTER 14

Swing Batter Batter Swing

You will be up to bat, take a few swings, and have some misses and strikes. You will be hit by balls that people throw at you. Sometimes, because they are hurt too, but also because the person throwing the balls has a demonic spirit attacking you. When God opens the door to leave a toxic workplace, you've hit a Grand slam, run to home, my friend!

Storybook endings are for Hollywood. It may not always go as planned, expected, or hoped. The important thing is you didn't sit it out on the bench; you went up to bat and gave it your best swing. Looking back, I was not perfect. Any less-than-stellar moments I have repented of and are now under the blood of Jesus. I had to learn to respond better to the disrespectful behavior and hurtful words of others. As a Christian, I did my best; there are many things I could have done or handled better. I believe many of those things were going to happen regardless. Looking back and knowing you did your best with the help of the Holy Spirit is golden! The result you will achieve, my Workplace Bestie, by taking God to work with you and being obedient to His leading, has eternal value; there is no end, only life & Victory. What I did get was an experience with God! I don't need the yellow brick road the world offers when I have a relationship with the one who made and gave me the streets of Gold. While I was crushed, I was not taken down; while I was disrespected, I remained. The word of God says I was pressed on all sides, 2 Corinthians 4:8. I weathered the storm and survived. I was kicked, dinged, and attacked. I have some wounds, but I had the armor of God on and was able to survive those hits because of the Armor of God, because what man meant for evil God turned into good (Genesis 50:20). I was kicked down, but I always got back up. I had to believe Psalm

MONIKA T. MORRISSETTE, MSW, LCSW

27:13 that I will see the goodness of God in the land of the living.

They ushered out truth and chose to believe a lie. I spoke the truth as I left. They thought I would go out quietly, and when I didn't, they decided to release me early, three workdays before my last scheduled day. I saw it coming based on being observant of their behaviors and words. Remember the devil overplays his hand, always. I knew my enemy and was prepared. The actions of these people indicated that they chose not to accept the truth, preferring instead to believe a lie. Seniority, longevity, hard work, and loyalty meant nothing. The Lord hardened Pharaoh's heart; the word says he gives rebellious people over to a reprobate mind. Those types of organizations are bound to fail due to their toxicity. They end up turning on each other; evil people always eat their own.

There has always been a catalyst in various areas of my life that I had to respond to, which seemed to move me to the next season of my life. In Matthew 5:25, it says, *"Agree with your adversary quickly, while you are on the way with him, lest your adversary deliver you to the judge, the judge hand you over to the officer, and you be thrown into prison."* The Bible also says in Romans 12:18, *"If it is possible, as much as depends on you, live peaceably with all men."* I want to say that when I left some workplaces, it went well; that wasn't the case, though, in other places. I made sure I left things physically clean and as organized as possible. I made every attempt to leave things better than I found or was given them.

All this I went through was for you. Because God sees you and knows you would need a workplace bestie, too. God sees how invisible, devalued, dishonored, broken, disappointed, and humiliated you are feeling. You are not any of those things. You are loved and valued. God sees you. He is Adoni El Roi, the God who sees.

Some Things to Remember:

- Give appropriate notice; even if they decide to "release you early," you did the right thing.

- Don't second-guess yourself when you tell the truth and it makes others uncomfortable

- Make every attempt to leave things better than you found them or were given to you

- Make every attempt to leave peacefully, but again, your employer may not be peaceful. You make sure you do the right and honorable thing.

- When you know better, you do better.

- Leave when God says leave, you could miss a lesson and Grace in God's timing!

"Therefore, we do not lose heart. Even though our outward man is perishing. Yet the inward man is being renewed day by day. For our light affliction, which is but for a moment, is working for us a far more exceeding and eternal weight of glory, while we do not look at the things which are seen, but at the things which are not seen. For the things which are seen are temporary, but the things which are not seen are eternal."

— 2 Corinthians 16-18

CHAPTER 15

You Can Do Hard Things

I realize I went through all of this for you, My Workplace Bestie. God gave me this experience, and not only did He see me through it, but He will also see you through. I used to think I didn't want to have to go through all this. I'm a Christian, and I am not supposed to have any problems because that's the thing we are taught when we become Christians. Everything is going to be great, everything's going to be better. The truth is, you have a target and bullseye that is put on your back when you start walking close with the Lord. Realize that when you want to go higher, you're going to experience some crushing things in your life. You have a choice to make. Do you want to stay where you are at, or do you want to grow? The Lord will enlarge your territory; in modern-day words, he will give you more capacity, "bandwidth," to move forward.

We can take things personally when we are hurt, and that hurt is exacerbated by our unhealed wounds. We want to live free. Everything people say should not open a wound. Receiving healing, restoration, and deliverance is needed. God can do it, he is Jehovah Rapha, God our Healer. We need to learn not to dismiss everything as simply taking it personally; it could also be a warning. If you listen, the Holy Spirit will help you discern the truth.

As a Christian, you do not have an ending; you have eternity with Jesus. While we are living in this world and not of it, there will be trials. However, you will survive and make it through, and God will use you and your experience for His glory.

You may be in the middle of the crushing and feel like giving up; persevere, keep going, and finish strong. If it's not good, God is not done; he will not leave you with nothing. The workplace challenges you're facing may be overwhelming, but like me, they won't kill you. I thought it would. You may be disrespected, dishonored, bullied, kicked, bruised, but it will not hurt you as long as you have the full armor on.

My workplace chose to usher me out three weeks after my resignation; they decided to usher out truth and believe a lie. Truth was spoken as I left. I suppose they thought I would leave quietly, and I mainly did, but I spoke the truth regardless of how unpopular it was. They will need that truth one day when they have to face the truth of their choices. People choose to be deceived and believe a lie. Sometimes things must happen this way. A toxic workplace will take away from you what you allow. Refuse to be silenced but speak when God says speak. For that knowledge, you need to make time to hear from Father God

Maybe it's time to leave that toxic workplace. Remember, Lot, Sodom & Gomorrah were not destroyed until Lot and his family left. Sometimes there's a catalyst that expedites your process. We will not understand, but God has your days already mapped out.

I'm convinced now that all of what I went through in the workplace was for you, my Workplace Bestie. Because God sees you. I did the hard things, and so can you. I needed a Christian Professional Woman to help me navigate a toxic workplace. God opened a door to connect with my mentor in the Women of Influence Network, which changed my life. Some things you get right, and other things you need to repent of and ask God to restore you so you can do better next time. It's a training ground for a reason; we have to learn and not shy away from correction. The Bible says wise people listen to correction. Keep your heart right and surrender what is not right. Root out any hurt and bitterness; it will only hold you back. Ask God to show you what your storybook workplace looks like, and what he wants you to learn and do.

Something to Remember:

- A final thought for you, My Workplace Bestie, You are Fearfully and Wonderfully Made, Psalm 139.

- Remember to keep the eternal perspective in the end, with Jesus, you win! And you will live happily ever after.

HOLD ON A MOMENT
I'm adjusting my Crown

"She will place on your head an ornament of grace; A crown of glory she will deliver to you" (Proverbs 4:9, "She" is "Wisdom").

CHAPTER 16

Hold Your Head High & Fix Your Crown:

Your Call to Action

I want you to be healed and delivered, and put your oxygen mask on, take care of your stuff, your heart, repent, and forgive. Assess the situation, determine what God is leading you to do, and do not leave too early; stay only as long as God has told you. Make sure you learn all the lessons, or you will have to repeat the test down the road.

I could tell it was time to go; things were shifting in a way that made me realize it was time to leave. A year or two beforehand, changes happened. It was appropriate to leave. I wanted to leave the team fully staffed, and I did. Give notice and be at peace as far as is in your power. Rebellious people will not have a drop of peace in them, so do not be surprised.

If you are leaving, get your personal effects out because they could be nasty and send you home, too. Be prepared to be sent home that day when you give your notice, so you can be proactive, not reactive. Be proactive so you are ahead of things. Know your enemy; they don't play fair, and when you do, you can prepare accordingly. Strategy... no one caught me unaware; they thought they did, but no. They underestimated me, but I knew my enemy and expected them to do just what they did in the end. That's why I prepared in advance and kept my plans to myself.

When you leave, you owe no one an explanation or 411 on anything you are doing. You are fixing your crown, do not allow the enemy to come and rip it off on your way out. I recommend not sharing any information unless necessary for your next employer. Do not give people who have partnered with Satan insight into your next move. I would even wait before posting on a professional website until you have passed the probationary period or even a year with your new employer. You owe no one

MONIKA T. MORRISSETTE, MSW, LCSW

information. You fix your crown by keeping your boundaries. Don't undo your hard work by spilling the beans or the tea.

Pray, fast, and receive downloads and strategies from God. Pray and sing in the spirit, using Scriptures and songs to encourage yourself. Your path may not be my path, but pressure and attacks are assignments from the enemy. Do not partner with the enemy in your destruction; you have value, worth, and purpose, and it is not dependent on whether someone else recognizes it. Whose voice will you listen to: the voice of people whom the enemy is using to destroy you, or will you listen to what God says about you? Agree today to speak what God says about you. Tell your story that the enemy is hoping he can steal, kill, and destroy. Shut the accuser of the brethren up by pleading the blood of Jesus! Speak life over your life. We overcome by the blood of the Lamb and by the word of our testimony, committing to speak life over your life, which is your testimony.

Call to action, so what's your story? You are not stuck; maybe a step of faith is needed to begin some momentum. Perhaps you need a catalyst, but it starts with taking a step of faith. Workplace Bestie, remember when we started, I mentioned that sometimes the problems are our issues, but they are never the entire issue with toxic workplaces. When you listen to Father God, are led by the Holy Spirit, and are healed, you can clearly see what was your stuff and what belongs to the toxic workplace culture.

Healing allows you to know the truth for what it is. This will help you move forward. Focus on your deliverance and healing, and put your oxygen mask on, take care of your stuff, your heart, repent, and forgive.

Assess the situation; what is God leading you to do? Don't leave too early, and stay only as long as God has told you. Girl, move aside, get out of the way, and allow God to part the Red Sea. Get up and out of that place!

You will know when it's time to move on. For me, things began to shift, and the company was changing. I paid attention to these changes. The call and anointing had been fulfilled. The Lord told me before I became too comfortable that this workplace was a training ground. So, years prior, the Holy Spirit had shown me that I would not be in this place for much longer. You will know, much like I knew, that it was time to leave a year or two before changes happened. God will always prepare you, but you need to hear him above the noise of the nonsense and foolishness. Yes, it's difficult because so much is vying for your attention and energy. God's timing is awesome when propelling us forward into something greater. It is something you can't make sense of, but you know that God's hand was there. You will see the grass is greener on the other side with the Lord leading and guiding you. Psalms 23 says, "*He makes me to lie down in green pastures.*"

My grandmother would always say, "*I'm holding on.*" My mother would tell me to "*Hold your head high."* Workplace Bestie, I'm telling you to hold on, hold your head high. This meant never giving up, never giving in, to the emotional harm caused by others. Remember the old nursery rhyme *"Sticks and stones will break my bones, but words will never hurt me."* We know the truth of how hurtful words are, having lived through and for some of you, continuing to endure toxic workplaces. The truth is, our flesh, our human parts, are hurt and harmed by the evil words spewed at us. But... as we learned, you will get pushed, crushed, dinged, kicked, and things thrown at you, including slander in your face and behind your back.

All that you are going through is an attempt to put out the light inside you. When we have the light of Jesus, it irritates those who have demons within them. People try to take your shine, but they can't take your light because you have the light of Jesus. They try to take your crown to dishonor and disrespect you, but your crown does not fit them. The truth is, they want your crown; do not abdicate what God has given you. Sure, you may feel like a hot mess at times, but you still have a crown of glory because you are the daughter of the Most High God, the King of Kings and Lord of Lords.

The fight you have been in, the toxic workplace(s) you have endured, may have shifted your crown, but it did not — and cannot — take it. That's why I say Hold your head high & fix your crown. How do you fix your crown? Well, we learned some things to remember and take away from each chapter. But the main one here comes from my pastor in Florida, Pastor Tim Gilligan. He says, *"I'm either up or I'm getting up."* I love this quote because you may have been kicked down, but get back up, shake the dust off, and fix your crown. The hurt and stress of your toxic workplaces shifted your crown in battle. When we get up, we dust ourselves off, fix that crown back into position, and be ready for your next assignment.

You may be asking yourself How do I hold on, how do I hold my head up high, how do I fix my crown. Great questions! I encourage you to do the following:

Hold On:

We hold on by identifying what gives us strength and power in a season we feel powerless: The only way through a feeling of powerlessness is to find our power and authority based on what the Word of God says. As Christians, we hold on by persevering through, fighting the good fight of faith, and trusting Father God. We hold on by knowing our value, worth, and authority, and exercising them with the help of the Lord, guided by the leading of the Holy Spirit. Begin to develop a list of go-to Scriptures that you can declare over your situation, workplace, life, and future. You hold on by knowing the spirit behind people, places, and things. Once you see it, you can't unsee it. Decide today to no longer be shocked by the behavior of people. We live in a fallen

world, pride, arrogance, and rebellion are on the

rise. If it's happening in the streets, it's

happening in the workplace, so it is what it is,

but it does not need to torment you. Pray for a

supernatural thick skin…it's the full armor of

God!

Hold your head high:

To hold your head high, you have to get

up. This is not a call to be arrogant and

prideful; remember that's nonsense and

foolishness. This is a call to get up if you have

been kicked down. If you feel you are in a pit,

you need to get yourself out, step by step, day

by day. Jesus took everything on the cross,

including anxiety, depression, overwhelm, and

hopelessness. Jesus' death, burial, and

resurrection, the finished work of the cross,
defeated death, hell, and the grave. So
Workplace Bestie, the resurrection power of
Jesus defeated all toxic workplaces. Call out to
God, and if all you can say is Jesus, save me and
help me get back up, he will. He did for me and
he will do it for you. Get yourself up, hold your
head high.

Fix your crown:

Living the life of a Christian is not easy.
In fact, maybe many of us were told, "Your life
will be better as a Christian." And it is, but it's a
fight of faith; there are tests, trials, and attacks
to endure. Why, well, sin entered this world
with Adam and Eve, and Satan influences this
world, but his time is short, very short. That is
why Satan sends evil people to wear out

Christians. This is why he uses weak-minded people to stir up strife, resist you, and attack you. Satan is trying to steal from you what he cannot get back when he decided to rise up against God Almighty. He can't take your crown, but he is trying to get you to abdicate your crown and give up. Do not give up! I was determined not to let evil win or steal from me any longer. We fix our crowns by tending to ourselves, healing our wounds, and preventing bitterness, offense, and anger from changing us or taking root in our hearts.

When you have been hurt, the tendency is to hide because you feel vulnerable, ashamed, unworthy, and too broken to do anything. I encourage you to identify what has been done or spoken to or over you that has impacted your life. Challenge those lies and talk about the truth of who God says you are. It all comes down to what you believe. Do you believe the lies that others said, or do you believe the truth? Even if some of what they said is true, no one is perfect, not even them. But, all your sins and shortcomings you put under the blood of Jesus, and they are covered. Only someone guilty will try to point out your flaws and sling mud at you. It could be their sins that are not covered. Now isn't that like Satan, the accuser of the brethren, to throw shade and sling mud? You fix your crown by speaking life to yourself. You fix your crown by not isolating yourself, but by moving forward with your life and not allowing Satan to steal your joy.

Thank you, Workplace Bestie, for allowing me to fix your crown as I allowed Jesus to fix mine in the process. I look forward to laying this crown at the feet of Jesus to bring honor and glory to what He has brought me through. Whether you stay or move on, I look forward to hearing about how your workplace atmosphere has changed. Looking to Jesus as the author and finisher of our faith. Now go out and change those workplace atmospheres to the glory of God!

Some Things to Remember

- Pray and fast get downloads and strategies from God daily!
- Pray and sing in the spirit, Scriptures, songs, and encourage yourself

- Do not partner with the enemy in your own destruction

- You have value, worth, and purpose; it is not dependent on whether someone else recognizes it

- Whose voice will you listen to? The voice of people whom the enemy is using to destroy you – instead, listen to what God says about you

- Agree today to speak what God says about you

- Tell your story that the enemy is hoping he can steal, kill, and destroy.

- Shut the accuser of the brethren up by pleading the blood of Jesus! Speak life over your life. We overcome by the blood of the lamb and by the word of

our testimony, commit to speaking life
over your life that is your testimony

- You are not stuck; maybe a step of faith
is needed to begin some momentum.
Perhaps you need a catalyst, but it starts
with taking a step of faith.

- You are fearfully and wonderfully made.
What man meant for evil, God will turn
to good.

- Make sure you heal, physically,
emotionally, and mentally.

- Forgive, do not become bitter,
offended, or ashamed in your next
season. Release it right now, release it
today! Do it by faith and do it daily until
that heavy stronghold is lifted. Pray for
your enemies.

- Pray for the Lord to enlarge your territory, capacity, and your "bandwidth"

- A word from the Lord to you that came to my heart as I wrote this book: There is an anointing on finishing.

A blessing for you!

Numbers 6:24-26 *"The Lord bless you and keep you; The Lord make His face shine upon you, And be gracious to you; The Lord lift up His countenance upon you, And give you peace."*

About the Author

Monika T. Morrissette is a Licensed
Clinical Social Worker with nearly 30 years of
experience in the social work field, spanning
various social services and healthcare settings.
She is a native California girl from the Golden
State who relocated several years ago to Florida,
the Sunshine State. She is a compassionate and
engaging counselor to many in their time of
grief, crisis, and adjustment to change. Monika
has worked with clients navigating chronic
health issues, end-of-life care, anxiety,
depression, and trauma. She is known for her
ability to easily engage those navigating
challenging situations and help identify

proactive solutions. She is known for not liking patch jobs and Band-Aids but getting to the root of the problem with real solutions. She meets her clients where they are and walks with them through life's challenges. She earned her Bachelor of Sociology from California State University, San Bernardino, with an emphasis in Social Work and a minor in Criminal Justice. Monika earned her Master of Social Work degree from Loma Linda University.

A transformed and proven leader who has navigated several toxic workplaces and endured them all with the help of the Holy Spirit to see the spirit behind people and their strongholds. As a leader, she has provided mentoring, coaching, and supervision to peers, colleagues, and students in the social work field.

Most importantly, she is a Christ follower, saved by grace through the finished work Jesus did on the cross. She is an overcomer by the Blood of Jesus and the word of her testimony, and she has a passion to encourage and empower others who need Jesus to lift their heads. She is passionate about encouraging those who need a personal cheerleader to help identify truth and expose the lies of the enemy that keep them defeated. Monika empowers others to challenge the lies they have believed and speak what is true about who they are in Christ Jesus.

Monika loves her family, friends, and her fur baby, Zoe, a Chihuahua Terrier Mix known for her charming, feisty personality and her oh-so-cute Chihuahua side eye. Monika currently works as a therapist in Ocala, Florida.

Monika is available for speaking engagements,

consultations, mentoring, coaching, and

presentations. For more information and to stay

in touch with Monika, please connect by

visiting my LinkedIn account at:

www.linkedin.com/in/monikamorrissette/

Book Summary

What would workplaces look like if Christian Women knew how to go about battling toxic people, places, and things? Toxic workplaces are being exposed when Christian women know their value, worth, and truth from lies. The exposure also occurs when Christian women recognize and utilize the power and authority they have been given as daughters of the Most High God.

Question for all the toxic workplaces out there: I've heard it asked, "Are you being careful how you play your cards when you have a queen in your hand?" I'm asking for a friend. Where there is a Queen, there is always a King;

the people you mistreat are daughters of the King of Kings. Remember that! Satan, with whom you have partnered, is running out of time.

In *Once Upon a Workplace,* I reveal that behind toxic workplaces are demonic strongholds used by Satan to steal, kill, destroy, and silence the voice of professional Christian women to ultimately attempt to hinder God's plans and purpose for their lives and the lives of others.

Toxic workplaces are a result of insecure, imperfect, unrepentant, and most likely unsaved people making the unfortunate decision to partner with Satan to create division, hindrances, stress, and disunity in the workplace. As Christians, we are in the world and not of the world. That puts a target/bullseye on your back. We can unknowingly give an open door to Satan to attack our lives through the strongholds and unhealed areas we show up with every day to work. It's time to learn what those strongholds are, to get your healing, and to live free the way God designed you to live.

Keep doing your best, but this time take Jesus to work with you. Can a toxic workplace survive a Professional Christian woman who knows her authority in Christ Jesus? No, it's a matter of time when lies and evil people are exposed and their nonsense and foolishness crumble like a house of cards. Workplace Bestie, hold on, you'll be out of there soon. God will never leave you or forsake you in a toxic workplace. You can endure, get through,

and live to tell about it!

Resources

For Christian Mentoring for Women:

Women of Influence

www.charlanakelly.com/womenofinfluence

For a Christian Counselor/Therapist,

look for one in your area at:

American Association of Christian Counselors:

https://www.aacc.net/

For information on Christian Counseling Services:

Above & Beyond Christian Counseling

https://www.aandbcounseling.com/

Focus on the Family

https://www.focusonthefamily.com/family-qa/how-to-find-a-christian-counselor-spiritual-professional-and-practical-considerations/

Biblical Counseling Center

https://biblicalcounselingcenter.org/biblical-counseling-and-traditional-talk-therapy/

Christian Counseling Services:

https://christiancounselingservicesaz.co
m/biblical-counseling-vs-christian-
counseling/

Lime Tree Counseling Services:

https://limetreecounseling.com/unders
tanding-the-difference-between-a-
christian-counselor-and-a-therapist/

*For more information on the difference
between counseling and psychotherapy,
refer to:*

American Psychological Association:

https://www.apa.org/topics/psychothe
rapy/understanding

Psychology Today:

https://www.psychologytoday.com/us/
basics/therapy/psychologist-vs-
therapist-vs-counselor

Please note: I recommend Christian Counseling/Therapy from a Christ-centered counselor/therapist who can provide talk therapy using Cognitive Behavioral Therapy techniques.

*For **general information** about Counseling and Therapy:*

Very Well Mind:

https://www.verywellmind.com/therapy-7092217

Bibliography

Public Sector HR Association:

https://pshra.org/the-boss-as-a-target-recognizing-and-stopping-upward-bullying/

Workplace Bullying Institute:

https://workplacebullying.org/2021-wbi-survey/